FROM PASTIME TO PASSION

Baseball
and the
Civil War

Patricia Millen

HERITAGE BOOKS
2007

HERITAGE BOOKS

AN IMPRINT OF HERITAGE BOOKS, INC.

Books, CDs, and more—Worldwide

For our listing of thousands of titles see our website
at
www.HeritageBooks.com

Published 2007 by
HERITAGE BOOKS, INC.
Publishing Division
65 East Main Street
Westminster, Maryland 21157-5026

International Standard Book Number: 978 -0-7884-1775-7

For my Meemon and PopPop Falcey
and Sean Hardman

TABLE OF CONTENTS

Acknowledgements

I would like to gratefully thank the staff of the National Baseball Hall of Fame Library and Museum for their professionalism, support and encouragement of the use of their archives during the research of this project. Most especially I would like to thank Mr. Tim Wiles, Director of Research, and Mr. Tom Shieber, Webmaster, for their assistance and sharing of materials. I couldn't have done it without them!

A heartfelt thanks goes also to the staff of the New York State Historical Association, Mr. Wayne Wright, Librarian, Mr. Glenn Linsenbardt, Staff Photographer, and most importantly to Ms. Deb McCaffery, former research librarian, for patiently tracking down many, many articles for me.

Thank you also to my friends and former co-workers, Karen Wyckoff, Daniel Beams and Ted Shuart for their motivation.

A special thanks to the publisher of my first book, Debbie Allen, of Black Dome Press and Steve Hoare, author, and also of Black Dome Press for doing initial readings of the manuscript and for assisting me in finding a publisher.

Thank you also to Andy Moye, Jim Sumner, George Kirsch and Mr. Tom Heitz for sharing materials and to Mr. Peter Harrington, Curator of the Military Collection at Brown University Library, for supplying some terrific images.

And last but not least to my husband, Brian, for his continued love and support of my research and writing.

Introduction

Long before the first shot of the Civil War was fired at Fort Sumter, South Carolina, the game of baseball had already entrenched itself into American society and was well on its way to becoming "America's National Game."

Writers have pondered the mystique of the game of baseball for decades. Many of these writers and historians have argued, or at least alluded to the possibility, that the game of baseball and its rise in popularity during the late 19th century was the result of the spread of the game by thousands of men from all over the country together for the first time during the American Civil War.

Standard baseball histories written by authors Robert Weaver, Robert Smith, and Albert Spalding, to name only a few, credit the War for the transformation of the game from a regional pastime to a game of national character with uniform rules and patriotic overtones. As sporting goods tycoon and writer Albert Spalding published in 1911:

For, during those years of unhappy conflict, on both sides of the line "Yanks" and "Johnnies" were playing ball and laying the foundation for a game which, when war's alarms cease, would be national in its spirit and national in its perpetuity.[1]

And Robert Weaver extolled in 1939:

During this conflict, ...the game became nationalized... When the soldiers were not fighting they played baseball; teams from different regiments frequently played games; soldiers from the North carried the game into Confederate prison camps; and Southerners came in contact with the game in Northern prison camps...[2]

Robert Smith reiterated the same findings:

...sporting gentry saw in it [the Civil War] the death of baseball, if not every game they knew. Yet the war was actually the means of making baseball a truly national game. It was played under various rules in every camp; and the New York game unquestionably proved itself the handiest and most efficient form...[3]

More recent publications have reached the same conclusion—even grammar and high school textbooks credit the War for the dissemination of the game of baseball. "During the Civil War the game spread when Union soldiers from New York taught soldiers from other parts of the country how to play,"[4] informs a high school text, while a grammar school book on the Civil War restates: "The soldiers had lots of time to play ball games in their army camps. After the war, they took the new baseball rules home with them and taught them to their friends and children."[5]

Bat and ball games were no revelation to soldiers in army camps, however. Ball games had been played by man for hundreds of years and were well known to men in the Union and Confederate armies who had grown up with a sporting heritage. The popularity of the game had taken hold well before the Civil War, advancing throughout the 19th century as America's favorite sport. The men from the Union and Confederate armies had marched off to war knowing how to play baseball.

By examining available sources on the leisure time activities of Civil War soldiers, it is clear that baseball was indeed played with great enthusiasm by northern and southern troops. Soldiers played in army camps, in winter quarters and while pausing in between marches. A detailed look at the daily activities of Union and Confederate soldiers during the War, however, reveals that baseball was played with far less regularity than other leisure time pursuits. Soldiers were too often consumed with the daily obligations of army life, and at times, consumed solely with the task of survival, compounded by fatigue and hunger, or just plain boredom, to engage regularly in baseball matches with their comrades.

Baseball *was* an important outlet for the soldiers, as were all sports that were played as an escape from the realities of the War. But, for the game of baseball to become truly nationalized during the War, Union and Confederate soldiers, or at least many different regiments from various states, would have had to have the opportunity to play *together and often.* Such was not the case. When soldiers did play ball, it was usually a spontaneous action enjoyed by men within their individual regiments when all the necessary factors of time, weather, space and safety were on their side. No doubt, fond memories of a baseball game played by friends existed in the minds of Civil War soldiers long after the War, but they existed together with memories of a package from home on Christmas, or a romping foot ball game, or an afternoon's swim after a long summer's march.

Baseball's link to the Civil War is a natural consequence of the nativist attitude that is interwoven throughout this country's history. Americans fought a Revolution to become Americans, held an American work ethic, spoke a universal language—Americans needed and found an American game. Then, the Civil War tore the country apart and Americans looked for ways to reunite it by finding good in the chaos of the four-year war.

Wanting never to be associated with the English game of cricket, the attitude of Albert Spalding reflected the view of many Americans who found the bond between the "American" game of baseball and the Civil War both healing and patriotic. As Spalding wrote in 1911:

> Baseball had been born in the brain of an American soldier. It received its baptism in the bloody days of our Nation's direst danger. It had its early evolution when soldiers, North and South, were striving to forget their foes by cultivating, through this grand game, fraternal friendship with comrades in arms... It healed the wounds of war, and was balm to stinging memories of sword thrust and saber stroke...[6]

Baseball was introduced prior to the War as America's National Game, but was knighted with the title during the early 1900s when a commission determined positively that the invention of the game took place on American soil. The inventor was a young lad who later became an American soldier and Civil War General—the infamous Abner Doubleday. Although proven to be false, these findings have ever since linked the Civil War and baseball together in history books. The conclusion of the committee, the testimonials of A. G. Mills, later president of the National League, and a Civil War veteran and friend of Abner Doubleday, have been republished countless times to verify the progression of the game by soldiers during the hostilities. The writings of Mills, and often quoted statistics of the number of teams who joined the National Association of Base Ball Players immediately following the War, together with Otto Boetticher's popular illustration of Civil War prisoners playing ball at Salisbury, North Carolina, have been used innumerable times to exaggerate the progression of the game during the War years.

Before any cannon was fired or rifle loaded, men from the north and south had been playing the game of baseball.

During the War, the "New York Game" did not sweep "like dysentery through the Army camps"[7] as folklorists have previously believed. The rules for "Base" had been published in the United States since 1835, and the rules for the New York version of the game of baseball had been around for over a decade at the start of the War. Historian Harold Seymour's reasoning was more logical when he determined in 1990 that "by the time of the Civil War the rapid spread of the Knickerbockers style [or New York rules] of baseball [had] manifested itself in both the Union and Confederate armies."[8] The game of baseball had been advancing steadily since the 1840s and more than likely this popularity was slowed by the four year interruption of the war, rather than accelerated by the intermingling of Civil War troops.

Baseball was played, however, at the very beginning of the War and it was played to the very end—often documented in diaries, journals, letters and newspapers not as a discovery, but as a commonplace occurrence. It was recorded in writing, scant extant photographs and a few images drawn by Civil War soldiers. But it was more often noted as a matter of course—routine as the weather, the writing of a letter home or the washing of socks. Just as George Rolfe, company B of the 134th regiment New York Volunteers recorded in his diary:

> *Morning clear and white frost. Mailed letter home. No mail arrive. No drills. Take trip up Racoon Mt. Match of Baseball 33rd. Mass. and Hookers staff. 33rd Mass winners. Health good, spirits high. Beautiful warm day.* April 13, 1864 near Chattanooga, TN[9]

One can almost hear the crack of the bat and imagine the dusty, weather-worn soldiers striking up a game just as they did on the grassy fields back home, and for a brief time, forgetting where they were and all the possible outcomes of what lay ahead.

This image is the only known photograph of a game of baseball being played during the Civil War. The Civil War soldiers are from Company G of the 48 New York State Volunteers at Fort Pulaski in Georgia. Although the figures are indistinct, there is no question a game is in progress between the buildings of the fort and the posed soldiers in the foreground. Ca. 1862-1863. National Baseball Hall of Fame Library and Archive, Cooperstown, NY.

C HAPTER 1

A SPORTING HERITAGE

The game of baseball, known by Civil War soldiers, evolved from ancient stick and ball games that were played in a variety of ways with an assortment of different rules. Primitive stick and ball games such as "one-hole-cat," "two-hole-cat" (also known as 1, 2, and 3 "old cat" depending upon the region and number of players), "stool ball," "base," "rounders," "feeder," "town ball" and "sting ball" were played for recreation in early America. Regardless of their names, these games had the same elements in common—a batter hit a ball and attempted to run to a base or goal before the ball was caught, or the batter was put out by being tagged with the ball. The name changed, along with slight rule variations according to the place it was played but for the most part the games were basically the same.[10]

In early America, the playing of games was often scorned by leaders in communities with strong Puritan ethics. Governor William Bradford, of Plymouth colony, on Christmas Day in 1621 was disturbed when he saw men "in ye streete at play, openly; some pitching ye barr and some at stoole ball, and shuch sports."[11] New England clergyman of the 17th century, Cotton Mather, cautioned that "laudable recreations may be used now and then but I beseech you, let those recreations be used for sauce but not for meat."[12] Despite such warnings, the desire for recreation by early settlers could not be squelched and simple ball games continued to be played and modified in colonial America.

1

The routine of daily life in early America centered around the basic need for sustenance dominated by the seasons and the weather. But the drudgery of everyday life was often suspended, at least in part, on Sundays. As one diarist recorded in his journal in 1753 while traveling through New York State, "...even at the celebration of the Lord's supper, [the Dutch boys] have been playing bat and ball the whole term around the house of God."[13] Regulations were passed in Dutch settlements in an effort to keep the Sabbath as sternly as their New England neighbors by forbidding such entertainments during the hours of worship. "Dancing, Card-playing, Tick-tacking [backgammon], Playing at ball, at bowls, and at ninepins..." were not permitted.[14] According to one account, laws were even on the books in the south as early as 1797 in the city of Fayetteville, North Carolina, to prohibit the organized play of baseball on Sundays by African-Americans.[15]

In the 18th and 19th centuries, Americans enjoyed recreation frequently interlaced with work. Early Americans found pleasure in the company of neighbors while working to build stone walls, clear farm land, during the fall harvests, at husking-bees, at barn or house raisings and at gatherings such as quilting bees. Children and adults fished, hunted, sleighed and skated. Contests of skill such as shooting and wrestling matches and horse races could be found at local taverns throughout early America, along with cockfights, dicing, billiards and card playing. By the early and middle decades of the 19th century, running and walking contests also became prevalent. Accounts often mention cricket as being played as well as football and "bat and Ball."[16] By the late 18th and early 19th century, base and goal ball were well known in the United States; the name baseball was becoming common between 1800 and 1840.[17]

As the game of baseball matured, *Harper's Weekly* began to question whether or not the game was truly understood and played in all parts of the country by the mid-19th century. The editors seriously doubted its popularity anywhere but in a "few great cities. ...Do young men naturally learn base-ball in Massachusetts, in Pennsylvania, in Wisconsin, and in Louisiana?" they asked.

A New York reader promptly replied in the next month's edition, "...For twenty years (which is as long as I can remember about it) base-ball has been a 'popular game' wherever I have lived...Who that has attended country 'raisings' does not know this, and dwell with a pleasant remembrance on the game of ball that was sure to follow after the building or frame was raised? But not only in the region named [NY] is base-ball popular as a game, but in parts of Ohio, in Northern Indiana, and in Michigan, I am assured it is played a great deal."[18]

Because various regions of the country were settled by diverse ethnic groups, some differences can be noticed in the preferred choice of recreational pursuits. The Dutch of New York loved ninepins, for example, while cricket was popular where Englishmen settled, and horseracing became a favorite sport of the wealthy Celtic, Southern gentry. Although travelers and writers of the time recognized that the northern and southern states in antebellum America were "significantly different places," marked by a culture and inhabitants that were vastly unlike,[19] recreational activities in the "old south" during the 17th, 18th and 19th centuries were not far removed from most Americans—even those of the 20th century.[20]

In the antebellum south, diaries, reminisces and travel accounts mention ball as being played since its settlement. Residents in the states of Virginia, Alabama, Louisiana Georgia and the Carolinas, for example, enjoyed dancing, hunting, fishing, barbecues and playing games of bowling, tag

3

and games that "were not unlike our modern baseball."[21] In Colonial Williamsburg horseshoes and quoits and bowling games were played along with a game called Pall Mall (a game similar to croquet), as well as a game called Trap Ball— a predecessor of the game of baseball.[22] Ball playing and rifle shooting were added to amusements during the early days of South Carolina with "ball-alleys" (for lawn bowling) found frequently through the interior parts of the state.[23] By 1841 the *New Orleans Daily Picayune* was reporting on the progression of the game of ball in the south:

> *Playing ball is among the very first of the 'sports' of our early years...who has not played 'barnball' in his boyhood, 'base' in his youth, and 'wicket' in his manhood?*[24]

Much has been written about the wealthy planter class of the south and their choice of aristocratic recreation— horseback riding and racing, fox hunting, dancing at balls and gambling at cards. Baseball was also played, although not as frequently, within the *distinctly aristocratic* plantation setting. One writer tells of tents that were spread under the branches of giant oak trees for the protection of the ladies while "polite stewards of the clubs" waited on the delicate fans that turned out to watch a game in 1859.[25] The majority of the white southerners in antebellum America, however, were small planters and yeoman farmers who made up a large "middle class."[26] This middle class cultivated fewer acres of farm land and most owned few or no slaves. It appears that all the social classes in the south, including people held as slaves, grew up playing forms of football and shinny, a form of hockey. Baseball was played by master and slave before any southerner enlisted to defend the Confederacy.

Comprehensive studies of slave life in the south document ball play as a source of entertainment among slave children living on southern farms and on large southern plantations during the 18th and 19th centuries. Simple rules and equipment dominated the types of ball games that were played. Slave children used sticks to get a ball in a hole or goal during games of "rolly hole" or shinny. Baseball was played, recalled a former slave in Kentucky, using a ball made out of yarn with a sock used as a cover. Sam McAllum, a slave in Mississippi, didn't "recollect any playthings...cept a ball my young master gimme."[27]

Levels of tolerance varied from farm to farm and plantation to plantation as to the appropriate interaction that was permitted between slave children and the sons and daughters of their white masters. But often children were allowed to interface as they pleased and so slave and slave-owner spent part or all of a childhood together playing in the woods, fishing or playing at marbles or ball. The rules are not always specified for the ball games that were played but most likely the games remembered as being played by slave children were variations of the of the games of rounders and townball played by southern whites.[28]

On an Arkansas plantation with over eighty slaves, lived James Henry Stith. He remembered:

They were playing baseball when I was born. There were boys much older than I was already playing when I was old enough to notice, so I think they must have known about it in slave time...

After the Civil War, Henry Baker recollected playing games of "townball" on a plantation in Alabama. "De way we played 'townball,'" Baker remembered in an interview after the War, "we had bases en we run frum one base tuh de udder coase ef de runner wuz hit wid de ball he wuz out." In North Carolina Elbert Hunter played "cat, which wuz like baseball now," he recollected, "only different."[29]

One of the earliest cited references to a game of baseball, however, was made during a military campaign before the Union was ever formed. At Valley Forge, Pennsylvania, during the Revolutionary War (1775-1783) George Ewing, a Continental soldier, wrote in his diary of exercising in the afternoon of April of 1778 and in the intervals he "playd at base."[30] Not long after the Revolution, baseball began to evolve as a spectator sport due in part to the inter-collegiate competition of the early 19th century.

Organized athletic competition began in the 1820s with an increase of inter-collegiate sports, and amateur and professional competition as the United States grew into an industrialized nation.[31] Before the end of the 18th century, however, young students were playing ball games at universities such as Princeton where Varning Collins recorded in his diary in 1786, "A fine day, play baste ball in the campus but am beaten for I miss both catching and striking the ball."[32] College authorities at Princeton were so convinced that baseball games were interfering with studies that they attempted to ban them in 1787.[33] Popular also at Brown University, a student attending in 1827 remarked with enthusiasm in his diary his memories of playing baseball.[34]

The first widely advertised collegiate contest ever held was between Amherst and Williams colleges on July 1, 1859. Billed as "Base Ball and Chess! Muscle and Mind!!" on promotional broadsides, Amherst won by a score of 73 to 32 with the help of a local blacksmith, as legend tells it, disguised as an Amherst student.[35] The teams played the "Massachusetts" game of baseball on a Friday and chess on Saturday. Several months later, Xavier (college) met Fordham and played by the New York rules.[36]

Like most sports played on college and university campuses—where there were players, there were fans. Sports in the early 19th century had developed from the occasional, local, spontaneous and often work-related recreational outlet into organized clubs and teams to play sports as separate and defined events.[37]

With the population in the United States shifting from farm to factory, new lifestyles were developing. Outdoor pursuits such as hunting, fishing, horseracing and other field sports were no longer readily available to many working Americans living in large towns and cities.[38] New forms of recreation were found through organized sports designed to fit into the different rhythms of city life. These organized sporting competitions produced a class of non-participants and baseball was a clear favorite to watch by mid-century—despite the warnings of such widely read papers such as *Harper's* whose editors warned the readership in 1860 that spectators would become a passive group of "pulmonary men and women...childless wives...dyspeptic men..."[39] Columnists continually expressed concern for urbanites who were criticized for their "addiction" to spectator sports.[40]

Spectator possibilities were afforded mainly in large urban areas—New York City and its boroughs, Philadelphia, Boston and Newark, the hotbed of baseball prior to the Civil War. New Englanders played mainly the "Massachusetts game," Philadelphia had its version of town ball and New Yorkers played the "New York game"—distinguished by its diamond-shaped playing field. There were rule differentials in all the forms, but by the 1840s the game of baseball had evolved into a game that any 20th century observer would have recognized.[41] On September 13, 1856, *Porter's Spirit of the Times* reported :

This fine American game seems to be progressing in all parts of the United States with new spirit, while in New York and its neighborhood its revival seems to have been taken up almost as a matter of national pride.

Matches are being made all around us, and games are being played on every available green plot within a ten mile circuit of the city.

In antebellum America the south was still primarily an agricultural region with dispersed populations and therefore lagged behind the north in the organization of formal baseball clubs and teams. Baseball was thriving in urban areas, despite dwindling public spaces, because a commercial spectator sport needed fans, transportation to move them and communication improvements to promote the contests. In the rural south, baseball was organized in cities such as New Orleans (where at least 7 teams were organized in 1860); Baltimore, Maryland; Washington, D.C.; and Louisville, Kentucky prior to the War. In Augusta, Georgia, in 1859, young men were encouraged to play the "noble and manly game of base ball...to toughen the muscles...and stir the sluggish blood."[42] Henry Chadwick, who came to be known as "The Father of Baseball" for his commentary on the game and as editor of the *Spalding Guides*, even attempted to form a baseball club in Richmond, Virginia, but his efforts were interrupted by the start of the War.[43]

Teams were also organized at points west prior to the start of the Civil War in Chicago, Cincinnati, St. Louis, St. Paul, San Francisco and other regions of the "Golden State" where competitors were playing the "New York Game." *Wilke's Spirit of the Times* in 1860 reported that the "...New York game, is the only style of ball playing at all encouraged in California."[44]

Several black teams were also organizing just preceding the Civil War. One team playing in the Long Island area of New York shared the same name as another New York team. A letter after a game in 1860 advised the editor of a local paper to correctly identify the team as the "colored Union Club" so the two could not be confused.[45] At least three other all-black teams were in existence in the New York area before and during the War—the Henson Club of Jamaica, LI, the Unknowns of Weeksville, NY, and the Monitors of Brooklyn. Reports of their baseball matches were carried in the *New York Anglo-African* as early as July 30, 1859—possibly the first published account of a baseball game by African-Americans. *The Brooklyn Eagle* cautiously billed a game played in October of 1862 by the Unknowns and Monitors as the first played in that city between players of "African descent."[46]

Newspaper coverage increased interest and enthusiasm for the game of baseball. By 1860 full-column descriptions of baseball games appeared and even smalltown weekly papers began irregular coverage before the start of the War.[47] The title of "National Game" made its first appearance in the middle of the 19th century with many commentators on American culture making clear the distinctions between baseball and other "foreign" games. In 1858, for example, a prominent Bostonian, comparing baseball to cricket wrote in *Atlantic Monthly Magazine*, "our indigenous American game of baseball" was "perhaps more congenial...to our national character, than the comparative deliberations of cricket."[48] And two full years before the start of the Civil War, in 1859, *Harper's Weekly* ran an article debating whether foot ball or base ball was America's National pastime.[49]

Blow by blow reports from baseball matches played outside city limits were also sent to be published in sporting weeklies—one author "thinking that [the readers] may wish to hear how the National Game of Base Ball is played in the country," detailed a spirited contest that was held in Geneva, New York. The article in *Wilke's Spirit of the Times* on November 17 of 1860 noted that the home team lost because of their "inability to bat swift balls."

9

As the game matured, principle clubs such as the Knickerbockers of New York City (1845) defined rules, and the expanding railroad system promoted inter-state rivalries and baseball tours. In 1857/58 the National Association of Base Ball Players was formed (primarily made up of players from New York, New Jersey and Pennsylvania) to monitor and regulate the rules of the game and to enforce baseball's amateur status. Prior to the outbreak of the Civil War, baseball was developing as a major sport to be played and watched in the United States. As the *Long Island Democrat* extolled in 1858:

> *It is only a few years that the game of base ball has been considered of much account; excepting by school boys, who played entirely different from the clubs organized for base ball playing. But now we have daily accounts of spirited contests in this healthy and exhilarating game, from almost every section of the country.*[50]

When the call for troops was announced by Union and Confederate presidents, it is clear the soon-to-be combatants knew how to play ball. Members of social clubs and sporting societies, farmers, professional men, journeymen, college men and young boys in the north and south hurried into military service. Fear and anxiety gripped the country as can be seen in the actions of leisure time participants. The New York Yacht Club, for example, canceled its regatta at the start of the War in fear of Confederate raiders. Colleges with inter-collegiate baseball teams postponed matches and the National Association of Base Ball Players cut their season short in 1861 as "the great game of iron and lead ball, between the loyal and rebellious states"—not baseball—was then engrossing all attention.[51]

C hapter 2

While Waiting for Sherman...

The average Civil War soldier in the Union and Confederate Armies stood 5' 8 1/4" tall, weighed 143 pounds and more often than not, was born, raised and worked on a farm. For many of these young men, whose median age was 24, joining the army was a great adventure and often it was their first trip away from home. Neither side figured they would be away too long—most were planning to return home after a few short months following a singular decisive victory. If the testimony of A. G. Mills (later president of the National League in 1882), and sporting goods tycoon and writer Albert Spalding is to be believed, many of these young soldiers from the north and the south marched off to war with a baseball and bat tucked into their knapsacks.[52] This romantic notion is repeated countless times, most stemming from the above accounts. If soon-to-be soldiers did pack the tools of play, they were quickly discarded.

Along with their weapons, infantrymen in the Union and Confederate armies carried a canteen, a knapsack with extra clothing, toiletries, a sewing kit, personal items—including photos, tobacco, perhaps a small Bible, extra food and at times, extra ammunition. Soldiers secured across the top of the knapsack, an oiled groundcloth for sleeping and extra blankets. After getting the feel for marching with this 15-25 pound load during the first year of the War, soldiers quickly learned to discard most of it—opting to carry what essentials they could stuff into their haversacks (small pouches worn slung over the chest) and into their pockets.

"Never in my life have I seen such a waste of property as could be seen in this road," complained a chaplain in the Union army during a march in 1863, "...blankets, overcoats, jackets, blouses, guns and ammunition, etc." littered the road from the army that traveled before him. "There ought to be something done to check this waste," recommended the chaplain, as he rationalized that the government should be responsible and detail supply trains to transport the army's surplus that accumulated while in winter quarters.[53] If soldiers had the time or energy to play ball, most likely they would improvise—using a broken wagon wheel or a fence rail for a bat and a nut or rubber ball wrapped with a sock as a baseball.[54]

The erratic demands of army life afforded both armies "down" time to pursue baseball and other sports in between confrontations with the enemy and during the long months spent in winter quarters. Except for a few campaigns during the four-year War, both armies usually stood idle from late November or early December until the spring thaw in April or May—waiting for passable roads and hospitable conditions for fighting. It was during these times the monotony of drilling, drilling and more drilling was broken by an occasional game of football or baseball.

With as much as 95% of a soldier's time spent in camp, not much changed in the routine of the soldiers from one campsite to the next. "The day goes by like all the others," wrote one soldier in his journal, "...drilling our men, eating our rations, and sleeping in our tents..."[55] As Private Richard Van Wyck of the 150th New York Infantry explained when he wrote home in 1862 detailing his daily routine, "At half-past five, the drums beat for us to get up." Van Wyck's company of soldiers ate breakfast, drilled, had most of the day off with

IN THE TRENCHES BEFORE PETERSBURG.

Of all the leisure-time activities of Civil War soldiers, card playing was the most common pastime for men in both the Union and Confederate armies. 1864. *Harper's History of the Great Rebellion.*

"exception of two hours between three and five, drill, we have leisure. Leasure is meant meal time or anything we choose to do."[56]

According to available sources, there appear to be no substantial differences in how the two armies spent this leisure time. Documentation found in letters and accounts from Union and Confederate soldiers mention a wide variety of leisure time activities that occupied a soldier's time in camp. Many waited anxiously for news from home, often reading and re-reading letters until they were worn smooth, or they spent their spare time returning letters to family and friends. Soldiers in both armies also spent their quiet hours reading books, magazines and newspapers or playing games of chess, chuck-a-luck, (a dice game), checkers, quoits, tenpins and dominoes.

Often bivouacked near a water source, soldiers also reported fishing as a frequent pastime. Union and Confederate soldiers also spent time swimming during the summer. A Confederate soldier wrote that his regiment looked "like so many puddle ducks in a barnyard stock pond" while he watched dozens of his comrades swim in a river during June of 1861.[57] For soldiers in the Union and Confederate Armies, however, frequently exhausted by drilling, forced marches, lack of proper nutrition and rest, research verifies that leisure hours were more often spent playing cards than any other activity.[58] Playing cards, illustrated with everything from military generals to half-naked women, were hot trade items among soldiers in both armies throughout the War.

While in winter quarters, most of a soldier's time was spent engaged in mundane tasks such as preparing and maintaining their living quarters. For soldiers of the north and south a good deal of time was spent making their quarters as homey as possible—often installing stoves and chimneys for heat and building rustic furniture with which to decorate. Large tracts of trees were cleared for the building of crude cabins and huts, and to winterize tents by stockading them with logs. These were the homes of these large armies for months at a time. Tremendous amounts of trees were also cut to use for firewood. It was clear from witnesses and surviving images where these masses of men had camped because of the barren scars left on the landscape. (Many extremely good images, both drawn and photographed exist to document these views, and can be found in the Library of Congress and other repositories)

For a good part of the sojourn in winter camp the weather was not conducive to outdoor sport—if it had been, the armies would have been on the move. Soldiers in winter quarters had few variations to their camp routines. They swept their living quarters, cleaned their guns, chopped wood, hauled water and washed clothing. For the men restless for activity on wintry days, ball games were often substituted with great snowball matches, some lasting the entire day! A soldier from North Carolina remarked that cockfights and snowball battles were the only things that made life bearable in camp.[59]

"...The air was filled with white missals," described a Yankee as a "notable engagement" took place between the 26th NJ and a Vermont regiment near Fredricksburg, Virginia, in 1863. "Stentorian cheers went up as one or other party gained an advantage..." The Vermont boys ultimately claimed victory when the New Jersey troops surrendered the field in defeat.[60]

Southern soldiers also released energy by "snowballing" when the snows began to cover their camps in November and December. Elaborate battle plans were often drawn, as men filled their haversacks with snowballs. Charges and counter charges were made, with prisoners taken when actions succeeded. Sometimes these battles involved an entire corps and were fought in territories covering ten square miles![61]

CAMP FORD, TEXAS.—SKETCHED BY G. W. SIMMONS.—[SEE PAGE 181.]

Civil War soldiers holed-up in close quarters in army camps such as these for a good part of the winter. March 1865. *Harper's Weekly*, The New Jersey State Library.

Ice baseball was a popular fad, especially in the New York area, during the 1860s and 1870s. Frank Leslie's *Illustrated News*.

Army commanders were not exempt from the divertissement—even General Robert E. Lee was admired for often taking part in the fun. A Georgia private witnessed a snowy-armed conflict in Virginia in 1862:

Sometimes the hole brigade forms, and it looks like the sky and the hole elements was made of snow...Gen Longstreet and his agitant took regs the other day and had a fight with snow balls but the Gen charged him and took them prisners.[62]

While the cold weather modified the leisure activities of soldiers in camp, it also adjusted ball play away from the battlefields. While the War dragged on during the winter of 1864, the Gotham and Empire Clubs played baseball—not on a field—but on the ice of Sullivan Lake in Hoboken, New Jersey. But, at the close of the second inning when the score stood 12 to 2 in favor of the Gothams, the parties hurriedly left the pond as the ice began to give way! The game was later adjourned to the New York City cricket grounds. (*New York Clipper*, Feb. 20, 1864)

Ice baseball began, like baseball, prior to the Civil War. One of the first written records of these peculiar ice matches was published in *Wilke's Spirit of the Times*. Four hearty teams—the Live Oak, Flour City, Olympic and Lone Star clubs—played baseball on skates on Irondequoit Bay near Rochester, New York on January 16, 1860. (*Wilke's Spirit of the Times*, January 28, 1860) Apparently amusing to watch and quite popular, these games drew large crowds. For example, thousands of men, women and children lined Litchfield's pond in Brooklyn, NY—many on skates themselves—to watch the Atlantics challenge the Charter Oak Club. The *Times* reported the game a "novel spectacle" and the first of its kind in Brooklyn. The men proved to be as good on skates as they were with bats and balls and reportedly

15

adopted the style of ice play from the Rochester area and other places where games on ice had been previously "indulged in." The Atlantics won the match 36-27. Ice baseball continued to be popular into the 1870s.[63]

Athletic games, including snowballing and baseball, became a way for soldiers in both armies to prove their manhood and to receive recognition in army circles. Team sports such as baseball and football demanded "physical courage and prowess"[64] and often times guaranteed fame for a soldier that might not be found on the battlefield. Soldiers won accolades for their ability to run, swim, hunt, shoot, box, snowball or play baseball even though their soldiering may have been less than admirable. John Adams, a soldier of the Union 19th Massachusetts, even came to view Confederate soldiers in a more favorable light after he witnessed their skill as baseball players. One Confederate was Frank Ezeel who was hailed in army circles because he could throw a baseball harder and straighter than anyone.[65]

Civil War doctors acknowledged the importance of physical exercise to the health of their men. Doctor Julian Chisolm, a published surgeon in the Confederate Army, wrote that while in camp, "Temporary gymnasia might be established, and gymnastic exercise should be encouraged as conductive to health, strength, agility, and address." The southern doctor was also familiar with and recommended the "manly play of ball" as an important addition to a soldier's daily exercise regime.[66] Such recommendations were made but soldiers, often lacking equipment and organization, made do with sport of a spontaneous nature by challenging each other to foot races, wheelbarrow races, wrestling or boxing contests.[67]

Union and Confederate doctors and officers also witnessed the affect of exercise and sport on the moods of their men and prescribed activity as an antidote for bouts of despair or

Harper's Weekly featured several illustrations of Civil War soldiers playing football, (a game that was played like soccer). One romping game was sketched by the famous Winslow Homer in 1865. Harper's Weekly, The New Jersey State Library.

homesickness. After the battle of Antietam, fought in Maryland on September 17, 1862 (the bloodiest single day of the Civil War), for example, commanding officer Francis Parker, of the 32nd Massachusetts, noticed a sharp increase in depression among his men as they remained in the vicinity of Antietam for nearly a month. He made several attempts to initiate games, team exercise or athletic contests to take his soldiers' minds off of their troubles—often it worked.[68]

Charles O'Ferrall, an Irishman in the 12th Virginia Cavalry, recollected the uncanny ability of sport to alter disposition. A soldier could be "bowed one hour in the deepest distress," he observed, and in the next hour be engaged in a horse race or other athletic activity. "Sorrow, remorse, fear, and despondency could be chased away, if only for the moment, by the gusto produced through sport."[69]

Newspapers also published articles on the benefits of exercise for citizens and soldiers. When war (or rumors of war) was the topic of most papers, *The New York Clipper* editorialized:

> *...would that every volunteer had been pupil of athletic exercises, gymnastic schooling, and pugilistic science ...we are sure that those whose muscular powers have been strengthened by a course of training, can now prove their superiority in every duty appertaining to a soldier.*

The *Clipper* later reported during the spring of 1862:

> *From all sections of the Union Army, we hear favorable accounts of the progress making in the introduction of sport and recreation among the soldiers. Some of the boys have become expert in gymnastic exercises, and others have accomplished some fast running. One young fellow made his mile inside of five*

minutes, and another, it is said ran one hundred yards in twelve seconds. *As it will take fast running to catch up with the rebels, we would suggest that pedestrianism should receive particular attention among the Union savers. (New York Clipper* May 25, 1861 & March 1, 1862)

The correlation between athletics and war was not lost with most of the sporting press.

Enlisted soldiers also found the relationship between the War and baseball a natural comparison. In April of 1864, for example, a Union soldier was camped with his regiment at Culpepper Court House in Virginia and was anxious for any kind of confrontation with the enemy. He remarked that, "if General Grant does not send them to have a match with Gen. Lee, they are willing to have another friendly match, but if he does, the blue coats think that the leaden balls will be much harder to stop than if thrown by friendly hands on the club grounds."[70]

The United States Sanitary Commission, a benevolent organization comprised of a philanthropic civilian core of men and women, was established in 1861 to oversee the health and well-being of the Union soldiers. Assembled from many of the local aid societies and overseen by its secretary, Frederick Law Olmstead, the USSC became the most important war relief effort in the country. Its capable agents supplied assistance in all forms to men in camp, in hospitals, and in soldiers' homes. It also provided funds to support widows and their children. The Commission recommended sport and exercise to benefit the Union soldiers. "When practicable," they concurred, "amusements, sports, and gymnastic exercises should be favored amongst the men, such as running, leaping, wrestling, fencing, bayonet exercise, cricket, baseball, football, quoits, etc..."[71]

This image details an array of leisure-time activities of Civil War soldiers including gymnastic exercise as can be seen in the upper right of the view. The 125th Regiment of the Illinois Volunteer Infantry is shown here, encamped in Tennessee.
Anne S.K. Brown Military Collection, Brown University Library, Providence, RI.

During the War, baseball matches were played on the home front with proceeds earmarked for use by the Sanitary Commission. A "grand match" was played on the Union Ball Grounds in Philadelphia on May 25, 1864, for example, between a New Jersey team and a Philadelphia team to benefit the local Sanitary Fair. And the Brooklyn Sanitary Commission was the benefactor of the profits from an exciting championship series played by rival teams, the Atlantics and the Eckfords, in the summer of 1862.[72]

One soldier wrote during the War that, "It was more fun to play base than minnie ball."[73] and the references to baseball games played during camp and in between hostilities by both armies are numerous. As Confederate soldier Corporal William Harding wrote while stationed in Georgia in 1863, "had a fine game of Town ball which gave me good exercise..."[74] Captain James Hall of the 24th Alabama Regiment observed his men playing baseball "just like school boys" while waiting for the advance of Union General Sherman.[75] The 13th Massachusetts played amongst themselves daily during April and May of 1862, while members of the 51st Pennsylvania played consistently each evening on their drill field.[76] Verification of such games in both armies seems to conclude that baseball was "the most popular of all *active* sports engaged in by Union and Confederate troops during the war."[77] When soldiers weren't playing poker and conditions were right, baseball was a favorite pastime.

But as documentation shows, most baseball games were as segregated as the army camps themselves, with ball games played most often just as they were at home before the War. Perhaps discussions took place before the game—whether to limit the number of runs to win, whether or not to allow soaking (hitting) the opponent with the ball or whether or not to catch the ball on the first bounce. If there were such

19

discussions, most were incidental. One soldier remembered in his diary that he and the boys from his company played ball with the 26th regiment from Pennsylvania in a "new way" but he had already forgotten the different rules. Twelve men from the 22nd Massachusetts challenged the same number of men from the 13th New York regiment to a game of baseball and they played the Massachusetts game.[78] Civil War soldiers were not overly concerned with the rules of play, they were only looking for a brief hiatus from the stress of the war.

While the War raged on, one question was put to rest, at least in one soldier's mind, concerning the homerun rules of the New York game. A sergeant from the 62nd N.Y. Volunteers wrote to *The New York Clipper* sporting weekly on May 30 of 1863 to clarify the rules as he knew them:

> *That in making a home run in a game of baseball* [NY game] *the runner is allowed to run 2' either side of the bases without touching them. I claim that he is obligated to touch each base as he passes it; ... To play now in N.Y. is to touch the bases in all cases; so that the matter is settled, and the rules can now be interpreted correctly.*

The rule differences did not seem to matter as much, however, as the ability to bat and field the ball. Soldiers remembered the ballplaying ability of some of the regimental teams as almost legendary. Charles David, of the 13th Massachusetts, and Thomas Aldrich, of the 1st Rhode Island Light Artillery believed or were thought to have believed, based upon their track record of wins in the army, that their teams could have beaten any of the professional teams of the 1890s.[79] The Civil War and the pent-up sports explosion that followed produced players such as Candy Cummings—the "Boy Wonder"—considered the inventor of the curve ball; Douglas Allison—Red Stockings catcher (and first to wear a glove); F. R. Boerum of the Philadelphia Athletics—first catcher to move up behind the plate; and Dicky Pearce of the Brooklyn Atlantics—first to drop a fly ball to produce a double play and eventually force a change in the rules.[80]

In the midst of the Civil War, businessmen were taking advantage of the moneymaking opportunities that the spectator market created. Two New York clubs, the Atlantics and the Enterprise, for example, announced in *The New York Clipper* that they would transform the Capitoline Skating Pond into the Capitoline Ball Grounds during the winter of February 1864. The enclosed field would allow for an admission fee of 10 cents to be charged on match days (hoping the future would bring more clubs to play if the grounds were properly maintained) making for "a great resort for the ball playing community." These businessmen were following in the footsteps of William Cammeyer of Brooklyn, New York, who drained his pond, filled it with dirt, nailed together some benches and enclosed the field in 1862 in order to charge admission on a regular basis.[81] Ladies and sports writers were often admitted free (perhaps as early as 1858) to help promote these early spectator rivalries.[82] The marketing possibilities were boundless, even during the War, to expand on the popularity of the game. The superintendent of the Coney Island Railroad teamed up with the Pastime Club of Brooklyn, for example, in May of 1864 to encourage tourists to take a rail ride to enjoy a ball game and to "sea bathe" all in the same day. (*New York Clipper*, May 14, 1864)

Occasionally, while opportunists were gathering fans to cheer on games away from the battlefields, games played by Civil War soldiers close to the action were witnessed by huge assemblages when rare moments made such spectacles possible. In Hilton Head, South Carolina, on Christmas Day in 1862, recalled Colonel A. G. Mills in 1923, his regiment, the 165th New York Infantry Second Duryea's Zouaves

21

"picked nine from the other New York regiments in that vicinity." Supposedly, the game was cheered on by a congregation of 40,000![83]

Such a crowd seems highly exaggerated, but large numbers of spectators were known to gather for such events. A correspondent to *The New York Clipper*, W. B. Wilson of the 2nd New Jersey Volunteers, for example, filed a formal complaint in the sporting paper when the "picked nine" of the 77th New York volunteers failed to show for a scheduled match. The no-show created "great disappointment" among the spectators assembled to watch in April of 1864. (*New York Clipper*, April 30, 1864)

Although the times when Confederate and Union soldiers fraternized were not as common as Civil War myth would lead us to believe, they did occur,[84] and there are a few known instances when a meeting (or confrontation) involved baseball. A game of baseball was played near Alexandria, Louisiana, for example, and was recollected in the writings of George Putnam. This game, played by men of the 114th New York, was interrupted by Rebel skirmishers who shot the right fielder, captured the center fielder and ran off with Putnam's only ball![85]

Albert Spalding wrote in 1911 that in the long campaign before Richmond, "at periods when active hostilities were in abeyance, a series of games was played between picked nines from Federal and Confederate forces." This scenario is possible but would have been a novelty. Even Spalding, as he continued to write of these games played in Virginia, admittedly remarked, "I have heard rumors of this series repeatedly, but have not been able to trace them to any authoritative source."[86]

Another rumor insists that members of Stonewall Jackson's second brigade were chasing a hare when they were joined by Union Yankees. An impromptu baseball game erupted on a

INCHESTER, VIRGINIA—THE FIRST MARYLAND REGIMENT PLAYING FOOT-BALL BEFORE EVENING PARADE.

Camp Johnson, near Winchester, Virginia - the First Maryland Regiment playing foot-ball before evening parade.

sunny hillside after the northern soldiers waved their hands to prove they had no weapons. Supposedly the southerners wanted to know how to play ball by the New York rules.[87]

Tyler's Farm in Virginia, in May of 1862, became a playground for the Irish Brigade attached to General McClellan's army while they rested after a muddy march towards Richmond. Football and baseball were played, and one Union soldier insinuated that *all the ruckus* being made "must have aroused no small amount of curiosity in the rebels waiting across the Cickahominy." A baseball game was played by members of the 57th New York and the 69th New York one Sunday morning on the Tyler farm. As with many calm moments during the War, reality often interrupted—the blast of a Confederate cannon ended the game abruptly.[88]

It was often on holidays that soldiers, north and south alike, had opportunities to relax and they indulged in sport as an alternative to their customary holiday celebrations. For example, a wheelbarrow race and a contest to catch two greased pigs rounded out the Christmas Day festivities for a soldier from Maryland, after he witnessed the officers of his company play three innings of baseball.[89] Soldiers held foot races, boxing and wrestling matches, and marksmanship contests, or challenged other regimental units to games of foot ball and baseball to fill the day when most soldiers were especially homesick and lonely for family.

Prize money was offered for a number of foot races held on the parade grounds of Camp Farm near Budd's Ferry, Maryland on New Year's Day of 1862. In the morning, the men were excused from duty and allowed to "ramble wherever their inclination prompted." Races of 200 and 300 yards took place along with a backward dash of 50 yards and a single dash race over a half-mile (for officers only) competing for a prize of $25. The race of 200 yards created the most merriment, however—its contestants were two 12-year-old drummer boys running for a $2 purse. Young Dobbins won the race by only a few feet and was "lustily cheered by the crowd." Some of the other boys amused themselves with games of football, baseball and cricket, while others put on exhibitions of the "manly art" (boxing?). The author of the article concluded that one result of the War "will be a largely increased patronage of outdoor sports." (*New York Clipper*, January 25, 1862)

Soldiers of the 2nd Brigade, 2nd division of the 2nd Corps of the Army of the Potomac, spent their Thanksgiving Day engaged in a "grand game of townball." Thanksgiving Day was traditionally the end of the season for ball play back home, with teams often made up by many who would not normally touch a ball all year but were looking for a "jolly good time" before dinner. During the holiday of 1863, twenty picked men from the brigade and some of the members of the old "Honey Run Club" from the Germantown, Pennsylvania, area reportedly played ball. The Honey Run Club made a name for themselves in the autumn of 1859 as champion players and continued practicing during their service in the Union army, intending to perfect their game. (*New York Clipper*, November 14, 1863, & November 28, 1863)

However, the majority of men during the War were more preoccupied with thoughts of the holiday feast they were missing than a game of baseball. *The New York Clipper* reminded its readers to "remember the vacant place by the fireside" and the "empty seat at the table" when it wished its subscribers a Merry Christmas in December of 1861. Many of the soldiers not on leave for the holidays, longed for a shipment from home so that their Christmas or New Year's Day meal would consist of more than boiled rice and lobskous—hardtack soaked with water and fried in pork fat. This unpalatable meal would have been prepared from the soldier's daily rations of about a pound and a half of salt beef

24

Camp of Battery B. 1ˢᵗ N.J. Artill'y Near Brandy Station Va.

This never-before published image shows the camp of Battery B of the First New Jersey Artillery near Brandy Station, Virginia during the Civil War. A baseball game is played on a diamond-shaped field in the right hand corner. This drawing was most likely done for a reunion of the Battery in 1870. National Baseball Hall of Fame Library and Archive, Cooperstown, NY.

or pork, their hardtack (or flour crackers), and coffee. Soldiers dreamed of butter and cheese and fruit and fresh vegetables when their funds ran out to purchase such luxuries from the sutler's tent. As John Haley of the 17th Maine wrote in his diary the day before Christmas, "It is rumored that there are sundry boxes and mysterious parcels over at Stoneman's Station directed to us...We retire to sleep with feelings akin to those of children expecting Santa Claus. We have become very childish in some matters—grub being one of them."[90]

Whether a holiday or a routine day in camp, ball games were played as one of the realities of everyday life during a man's stay in the army. Most of the games were consistently played between regiments from the same area of the country, and most were documented as being played by northern teams in areas where baseball had already organized into a major spectator sport. The 8th and the 114th Vermont played a game near Franklin, Louisiana, for example, while the 9th New York beat the 51st New Yorkers during a stop in Virginia. And the 13th Massachusetts scored 66 runs to the 20 made by the 104th New York during a lively wartime match.[91] There are many examples in Civil War journals and diaries, especially in the large collections of materials still extant from Union writers. But whether recorded as being played in the north or south, baseball continued to grow in popularity and, at the War's end, it continued to grow as all leisure time activities were blossoming in the developing, urbanized American society.

One never-before published image, apparently drawn from memory in 1870 for a soldier's reunion, depicts soldiers playing ball near Brandy Station, Virginia. The image shows the details of a game played among the men from Battery B, First New Jersey Artillery recruited from Newark, New Jersey—a region with a long history of baseball. The author of the memoirs of the artillery company, Michael Hanifen (a "wild Irish boy" from Trenton, New Jersey), recorded the game as possibly seen in the image shortly before the battery was engaged at the Battle of Chancellorsville in 1863. A game between the "first 9" of the 1st New Jersey and the 10th Massachusetts was also recorded in *The New York Clipper* as being played near Brandy Station on May 14, 1864—the 1st New Jersey losing 13 to 15.

Michael Hanifen, typical of most soldiers during the War, recalled one afternoon of ball as commonplace and without circumstance:

> *It rained some during the day, regular April showers. The men amused themselves jumping, wrestling, running three-legged races. One lot was playing ball. At night there was a quiet drizzling rain.*[92]

Union and Confederate soldiers who had been brought up with baseball continued to play for relaxation during the War. Like all leisure time activities, it helped the soldiers endure terrible hardships. Most soldiers, however, because of the realities of life in the army, never played baseball with any regularity for any length of time and only a handful actually ever played in prison camps.

C hapter 3

In Prison Pens...

"For months," wrote former prisoner Willard W. Glazier in 1866, "Salisbury was the most endurable prison I had seen; there were 600 inmates. They were exercised in the open air, comparatively well fed, and kindly treated. Early in October, 10,000 regular prisoners of war arrived. It immediately changed into a scene of cruelty and horror; it was densely crowded, rations were cut down and issued very irregularly; friends outside could not even send in a plate of food..." Willard continued that the prison "became so notorious during the War as one of the most loathsome dungeons in rebeldom..."[93]

This description illuminates the brief time that baseball could have been played in the pastoral surroundings depicted in the famous print of the prison at Salisbury, North Carolina. The popular print is often used to underscore how baseball was frequently played in prisons during the War while Confederate or Union guards looked on and took mental notes of the game. The reality of the image of the prison at Salisbury is that baseball *was* played and played almost daily—but for only a very short time while the rare conditions existed to make it possible.

The old cotton factory, turned prison camp, rested on 16 acres of land in the middle of one of the most populous towns in the Confederacy. It was purchased by the Confederate government for $15,000 and quickly renovated to accommodate the first prisoners who arrived from Raleigh in

December of 1861.[94] Not all the men at Salisbury were Union soldiers, however. The prison held, throughout its history, Yankee and Confederate deserters, convicts, civilian prisoners, soldiers held as hostages and approximately 300 Negro prisoners of war.

While the population of the prison remained low during the spring and summer of 1862, baseball games were played in the park-like grounds and recorded by Otto Boetticher, a commercial artist from New York City (originally from Prussia). Boetticher enlisted in the 68th New York Volunteers, a largely German regiment, at age 45. He was mustered in as captain of Company G on August 14, 1861. There was no fighting recorded during the time the regiment was attached to the Army of the Potomac when Otto was captured in 1862. He was sent to Libby prison in Richmond, Virginia, before being shipped to Salisbury. He remained there for only a summer before being exchanged for a Confederate captain on September 30, 1862. He was later discharged from service on June 9, 1864, with a brevet as lieutenant-colonel for "gallant and meritorious conduct." His image of the prison at Salisbury, "drawn from nature," was published in color in 1863 by Goupil and Company Lithography of Sarony, Major and Knapp of New York.[95]

We know of the baseball games drawn by Otto Boetticher at Salisbury from the diaries and letters of several Union prisoners and from the writings of a Confederate chaplain who resided in Salisbury. Before the great influx of prisoners shipped to Salisbury in October of 1864, the prison population remained relatively low. Designed to house about 2,500 men, Salisbury's buildings and grounds were comparatively spacious with the prison population shifting from about 800 to 2,000 men during the spring and summer of 1862. With the weather warm and the guards allowing the "liberty of the

The Confederate Prison Camp at Salisbury, North Carolina Lithograph of Sarony, Major and Knapp. Artist and former prisoner at the camp, Otto Boetticher drew this image of a baseball game in the park-like grounds of the prison. The lithograph distorts the reality of the horrors of the prison that the majority of the men experienced. 1863. Anne S.K. Brown Military Collection, Brown University Library, Providence, R.I.

yard" by the prisoners, some of the men enjoyed afternoon and evening games of baseball while imprisoned at Salisbury. [96]

"Took a little walk in the evening and watched some of the officers play ball," wrote twenty-three year old Charles Gray who was captured and sent to the prison in May of 1862. A Union doctor, Gray remained a spectator of the games at Salisbury and mentioned them frequently in his diary:

> *A good state of cheerfulness (sic), thanks to the open space is fairly prevailing. Ball play for those who like it and are able, walking, card playing as keep us in employment; but reading matter is about used up.* [97]

Gray (and other observers), after watching "match games" between teams such as the "New Orleans" and the "Tuscaloosa boys," and other games, noted that the "cells of the Parish Prison were unfavorable to the development of the skill of the 'New Orleans Nine'" which resulted in the Alabama team taking the lead. Apparently the conditions at the prison, where the soldiers from New Orleans were held, were not prohibitive to the practice of outdoor sport.

William Crossley, a soldier from Rhode Island, arrived at Salisbury in March of 1863. Crossley also accounted for a game played by recently transferred prisoners from New Orleans and Tuscaloosa, Alabama:

> *And to-day the great game of baseball came off between the Orleanists and Tuscaloosans with apparently as much enjoyment to the Rebs as the Yanks, for they came in hundreds to see the sport, and I have seen more smiles to-day on their oblong faces than before since I came to Rebeldom, for they have been the most doleful looking set of men I ever saw and that Confederate gray uniform really adds to their mournful appearance. The game was a tie, eleven each but the*

29

factory fellows were skunked three times, and we but twice.[98]

Who the factory boys were that Crossley refers to is not clear. Because the prison was on the site of a former factory, perhaps he was making reference to soldiers housed within the buildings on the site or possibly even Confederate guards. As historian Jim Sumner notes in his research, however, no other references to Confederates playing ball within the grounds of Salisbury have ever been found.[99] The one exception is in the writings of Josephus Clarkson, a Boston ship chandler's apprentice before the War.

In his diary, Josephus Clarkson recalled how a Union prisoner at Salisbury picked up a pine branch that was on the ground while another soldier wrapped a few stones in a pair of woolen socks and tied them with string. A casual baseball game was played after a lengthy debate over whether to play by the town ball or by the New York rules. Clarkson wrote of the occasion:

> *To put a man out by Town Ball rules you could plug him as he ran. Since many of the men were in a weakened condition, it was agreed to play the faster but less harsh New York rules, which intrigued our guards. The game of baseball had been played much in the South, but many of them [the guards] had never seen the sport devised by Mr. Cartwright. Eventually they found proper bats for us to play with and we fashioned a ball that was soft and a great bounder.*[100]

Clarkson later wrote that the prisoners repeatedly had to remind the guards of the New York rules and not to "plug" the runners on the opposing team. One pitcher from Texas was pulled from a game by consensus after "badly laming" too many of the prisoners. "We informed our captors," Clarkson

" He was shot through the lungs, and laid near the dead line writhing in torments during most of the forenoon."

A dying prisoner who crossed the dead line of a Confederate prison during the Civil War. 1867. Author's Collection.

remembered, "rather politely, or course, that we would no longer play with a man who could not continue to observe the rules."[101]

It may be surmised that the Confederate guards, whether they regularly played ball or not, must have enjoyed watching the games. One account written by Adolphus Magnum in 1862, the Confederate chaplain who visited the prison, described a dress parade at the prison at Salisbury:

> ...the officers among the prisoners came out and presented truly a beautiful scene in their recreation. A number of the younger and less dignified ran like schoolboys to the play ground and were soon joining in high glee in a game of ball. Others...sat down side by side with the prison officials and witnessed the sport.[102]

Magnum also recalled how prison soldiers played ball to celebrate the Fourth of July. They also ran sack races, foot races and blindfolded wheelbarrow races. Such memories were few, however, for the majority of the men imprisoned at Salisbury. For soon, as the prison population began to grow and after the great influx of prisoners into Salisbury in the fall of 1864, the conditions became unbearable.

Salisbury had all the earmarks of a Confederate prison from the beginning, not noticed by many until it felt like a prison in every sense of the word. Like all Confederate camps, it was enclosed by a 15 foot high stockade fence built around the exterior of the camp and a "dead line" trench that marked the distance between the fence and the prison yard that was not to be crossed by inmates. If anyone did get too near or cross the line they would be immediately shot by the guards, a sad form of suicide that desperate prisoners took advantage of when conditions were unendurable.

Rations at Salisbury, toward the end of its existence, were intolerable and meager. They were not substantial enough to support most soldiers for very long, especially when the lack of food was compounded by the lack of shelter, heat and medical attention. One soldier described the not always daily fare at the prison in 1864 as consisting of "coarse meal, cob and all ground together, and so musty that a decent hog would not eat it." Benjamin Booth recalled that he received about three pints of this ration of food during the first week he was imprisoned at Salisbury. The bread that was eventually baked for the prisoners (baking facilities were added later), was made using two parts sour milk and one part water in which corn cob ashes had been soaked to be used as a rising agent. The men at the prison referred to the bread as "limed" bread or "solid shot." Booth recollected the bread was "strong enough to make soap."[103]

Soldiers in the field, as well as in prisons, continually looked for ways to supplement their rations. Scavenging was a commonplace occurrence, only in prison, soldiers had no where to go and many times when hunger took over, would eat almost anything. There are many accounts of soldiers eating rats to survive and unfortunately, the supply was plentiful. Rumors and reports of dogs and cats also being eaten at Salisbury were not uncommon. A prisoner named Hubert Estes recorded a cat and a dog that "turned up missing" on the morning of December 2, 1864. In the South during the War, Yankees were getting a reputation for this behavior as illustrated in the *Richmond Inquirer* where a notice warned residents that valuable dogs should be watched closely otherwise Yankee prisoners would "instantly" devour them.[104]

In the end at Salisbury, death took almost a third of the men who entered her gates from October of 1864 until General Grant negotiated the exchange of the soldiers in February of 1865.* The buildings at Salisbury held no refuge for the men sent there, the main building had been converted into a hospital and outbuildings took over the daily operations of the prison—the old blacksmith's shop was used as a holding place for the dead. So, without food and warmth, thousands of men did not survive imprisonment—the best estimate would tally almost 4,000 dead. When the Union Army marched into Salisbury on April 12, 1865, three days after General Lee surrendered to Grant at Appomattox, it is not surprising that Union General George Stoneman ordered the prison burned to the ground along with a fair portion of the city itself. It is said that flames and explosions were seen and heard for 20 miles.[105]

Most of the memories of Salisbury prison then, were more likely to conjure images of horror than of a peaceful game of baseball as depicted in the print drawn by Otto Boetticher. One of the extant prints of the prison at Salisbury was advertised for sale in "Christie's East Sports Memorabilia Auction Catalog" in September of 1996. It was described as a propaganda piece, some modern dealers theorizing that it was produced to dispel the "myths" of the atrocities in Confederate prison camps. The estimated number of surviving prints is small, one collector claims that only 7 are known to exist north of the Mason/Dixon line.[106] But, for whatever reason Otto Boetticher drew the bucolic afternoon of baseball at Salisbury, history documents what life was truly like for most of the prisoners held there.

Life was not much better for many Confederate soldiers held in northern prisons. The Union prison at Elmira, New York, for example, has a cruel history all of its own. But even in northern prison camps, when conditions were tolerable, baseball games were occasionally played.

There are a few accounts of Confederates playing ball while being held on Johnson's Island, a 13-barrack prison and yard on a small inlet on the southern part of Lake Erie near Sandusky, Ohio. One southern team that continued to play after the War supposedly learned the "New York game" from their Union captors.[107] A closer look reveals that the Southern Baseball Club were all "southern men" and organized during the War while they were held prisoners on Johnson's Island. After the War, in 1869, they were looking to attract matches after winning the championship that same year in Louisiana. The team announced in *The New York Clipper*, a baseball tour beginning in August of 1869 modeled after the "victorious 'Red Stockings'" excursion.

Members of the Southern Club intended to travel to Memphis, St. Louis and possibly Cincinnati. The team didn't mention learning the New York game while in prison, rather, they wanted to be "induced to visit New York and measure skill with the Atlantics and Mutuals," and questioned, "...would it not be pleasant to see the hatchet buried in the great national game, spite of the efforts of politicians to keep up ill feeling between the sections?" (*New York Clipper*, July 17, 1869)

Another account, recorded in the writings of 1st Lt. William Peel of the 11th Mississippi Infantry Regiment, also gives the impression that the game was already well enough known by the southern prisoners. A 23-year-old farmer, William was captured at the battle of Gettysburg (July 1863) and sent to the Union camp for Confederate prisoners at Sandusky. He wrote several entries in his journal that detail games of ball:

29 July, 1864

There came near being a serious accident in the yard this evening. There was a party engaged in a game of baseball. The man at the bat struck with all his might, but missed the ball and the bat--a very large one--flew out of his hands and struck Cap't Fellows, who stood a few feet from him, plump in the forehead. The Cap't uttered a low exclamation, threw both hand[s] to his head, staggered and would have fallen to the ground, but was caught by a gentleman near him. He lay quite insensible for several minutes, but bashing his head at length revived him. The square butt end of the paddle struck him and consequently left no cut, but his head must be badly bruised. Leaning on the shoulders of a couple of friends, he walked, after a while, to his Block.

On August 28, 1864, William reported:

There has been, for several weeks, a challenge pending over one of the baseball clubs.
The Confederate Club Challenged the Southern Club. The game came off today and created more excitement than anything has done in the yard for a long time. There were several hundred dollars bet on the game by the clubs and outsiders.
They played nine innings. The Southerners beat the Confederates very badly: the Rounds standing nineteen to eleven.[108]

Lt. Peel wrote of the baseball games in prison as nothing new and he did not mention the Confederates learning a new game. Like most soldiers held in prison or involved in combat during the Civil War, William died from disease, not from the ravages of a minnie ball. He passed away from pneumonia on February 17, 1865, and is buried on Johnson's Island, grave number #129.[109] Many of his comrades, though, who survived the War, went home and continued to play baseball for recreation.

*The number of actual deaths at Salisbury is difficult to determine because most of the records were destroyed when the prison was burned. Even in Brown's **The Salisbury Prison: A Case Study of Confederate Military Prisons** (see* *pages 119 and 135), the numbers vary between a third and one half of the men sent to Salisbury who died between October of 1864 and February 1865.*

C hapter 4

On the Homefront with "Baseball on the Brain..."

"There is but little to chronicle in the way of sporting events this season," reported *The New York Clipper* in June of 1861. "Many of the most active participants in sporting matters have enlisted in the defense of the Union, and are now either at the seat of war, or preparing to march thither at short notice. Cricket and Base Ball clubs, usually so busy in the field at this period of the year, are now enlisted in a different sort of exercise, the rifle or gun taking place of the bat, while the ball play gives place to the leaden messenger of death..." (*New York Clipper*, June 22, 1861)

Despite the initial set-back caused by the onset of the Civil War, the *Clipper* and other sporting papers continued to routinely cover ball play along with other athletic news. The *Clipper* and *Wilke's Spirit of the Times* reported matches between the Eckfords, the Atlantics, Charter Oak and the Excelsiors—all from Brooklyn, as well as games played by the Mutual, Gotham and Union Clubs of New York—to name just a few. The *Clipper* also encouraged and announced the formation of many junior clubs to fill some of the baseball voids caused by the War.

The ball season of 1861 wasn't as dreary as the *Clipper* initially speculated. The presence of many spectators at local matches energized sports writers and convinced them that the popularity of the national game had not been diminished by the "pomp and circumstance" of the War. In fact, even as the War continued, ball play in major cities, such as Philadelphia, was "flourishing." In the City of Brotherly Love, *The New York Clipper* reported that, "All clubs muster well on practice days, and new ones are organizing." The *Clipper,* by November of 1863, concluded that despite the hardships of the War, the season of 1863 was a "brilliant one" and that soldiers were playing ball as well, with some "first class games" played in southern states during the War. The paper theorized that because of the adoption of the game by the army, baseball became naturalized in every state of the Union, so the baseball fever that began in 1858 reached its high point at the end of the War. The whole country, it reported by 1865, had "base ball on the brain." (*New York Clipper*, June 15, 1861, May 30, 1863, November 28, 1863 & April 12, 1865) It is difficult to support this theory, however. *The New York Clipper* was published in New York and the reporting of games in their columns is overwhelmingly focused on games played in the northeast before, during and after the War.

In Washington, D.C., the Nationals baseball club survived the war years and played, at times, to crowds of fans behind the White House. The 71st New York Guards, who were later annihilated at Bull Run, stopped to play the Nationals in Washington in 1861. And the 133rd New York Volunteers picked a match with the Nationals on their way home from Appomattox at the close of the War. The Nationals went on to tour the mid-west in 1867 stimulating even more interest in baseball, especially after they went nearly undefeated during the entire tour. The Rockfords, of Illinois, managed to tally a win over the Nationals—due in large, to the pitching of a seventeen year old named Albert Spalding.[110]

Supposedly, Andrew Johnson even witnessed the Nationals play in 1865 as they took on the Brooklyn Athletics and the

Philadelphia Athletics—possibly the first president to observe an inner-city tournament.[111]   Another story reveals that Abraham Lincoln may have been an admirer of baseball before Johnson succeeded him in office. Traveling with his son Tad, Lincoln is rumored to have watched a game held on the old Washington circus lot in 1862. Recollected by Winfield Scott Larner in 1914, President Lincoln, taking his son's hand, "modestly and unobtrusively...made his way up to where he could see the game and sat down in sawdust left over from the late circus." Sitting along the first-base line, the President watched the game while holding Tad between his knees and sometimes cheered like "the most enthusiastic fan of the day." Upon leaving, the President and his son "accepted three loud cheers from the crowd."[112]

While the war dragged on many teams still played, although they were fewer in number and the matches were not as frequent. The National Association of Baseball Players also continued to meet, amend rules and grow during the War. The Association held it first convention in New York City in May, 1857. Negotiations solidified the Association's rules during the winter of 1857 and 1858. Their goal was to "foster and extend this most popular of all American pastimes, until the National Association game is unanimously adapted throughout the land." (*Wilke's Spirit of the Times*, January 15, 1861)

The game rules endorsed by the National Association were fundamentally the "Knickerboker code" or the game rules and code of conduct put into writing by Alexander Cartwright's well-known Knickerbockers club of New York. By 1857 these rules, adopted by the Association, called for a diamond-shaped playing field, a nine-inning game, (ending the old 21-aces regulation that was previously required for a team to win a match), and rules such as those that forbid players to catch the ball with their hats or caps.[113]

Members of the Association were expected to be proper gentlemen with some degree of social standing. Would-be ball players had to be able to afford the uniforms, dues, grounds maintenance fees and the fines levied if they missed a membership meeting or if they used profanity. Teams often padded their membership rolls to include the names of famous Americans. The Empire Club of New York, for example, listed among its members the infamous Union General William T. Sherman and General Fred Benteen.[114]

Membership in the National Association of Base Ball Players started with 22 clubs in 1858, growing to almost 50 clubs in 1859. It wasn't until the 1859 annual convention of the Association that membership included teams outside New York City and Brooklyn. By 1861, 56 clubs belonged to the Association, representing New York, New Jersey, Pennsylvania, Connecticut, Maryland, Michigan, Massachusetts and Washington, D.C. Of the 56 teams, the overwhelming majority joining the Association were still New York clubs—36 from New York City and its boroughs, alone, along with 10 teams representing other regions of the state, such as Newburgh and Buffalo. Only delegates from a single representative club from Washington, D.C., Baltimore, Detroit, Boston and Connecticut traveled to New York to take part in the 1861 meeting. (*Wilke's Spirit of the Times*, January 15, 1861)

The National Association remained the formal promoter of baseball as well as a watchdog of the non-professional status of the game. Rule amendments were approved and adopted for its members—several of the major rule changes were made during the Civil War. The committee on rules, for example, discussed in great length among its members whether or not to adopt the "fly game" (catching the ball in the air) at the convention held in December of 1863. Most baseball players were still catching the ball on the first bounce or "bound" and many wanted it to stay that way. The question was put to a vote but the fly game was not approved at the Association's meeting. It was interesting to note, according to the report of the election, that the majority of the negative votes were cast by players belonging to the "muffin fraternity" (a name for third rate players), whose "fun," *The New York Clipper* editorialized, would stop altogether if the fly game was adopted. (*New York Clipper*, December 19, 1863)

Discussions continued into 1864 and 1865 concerning the rules of the fly game. The Association suggested trying it out for a season before formally amending the rules. By March of 1865, the press reported that the "prejudice" against the fly game was fast disappearing among ball teams. Balls hit during baseball games could then be caught either way— either the fly catch or the bound would put a player out according to the 19th century rules. (*New York Clipper*, March 25, 1865)

The Association also debated pitching rules (requiring pitchers to throw within a "legitimate" reach of the batter), and scoring rules were changed during the War years. The Association "heartily" recommended the scoring and averaging system detailed in *Beadle's Dime Book of Baseball* edited by Henry Chadwick and first published in 1860. They also waived their requirements, with regard to the number of players required to send delegates to meetings, in order to boost membership during the turbulent War years. (*New York Clipper*, May 14, 1864 & December 19, 1863)

Fluctuations in attendance to the Association's meetings during the War did occur. The season of 1861 witnessed a drop from the 56 teams in January of 1861 to 34 in attendance at the New York meeting the following December. The Association remarked on the "depressing influence" the War held on all outdoor sports but was hopeful that the National game would survive the trying ordeal. (*New York Clipper*, December 21, 1861)

The Association and the game did survive, and membership grew to 91 member teams in 1865, the last year of the War. Many decades afterwards, the convention of 1865 was triumphantly compared as "truly a sequel of Appomattox as negro suffrage and radical reconstruction."[115] In December of 1865, the Northwestern Association of Base Ball Players formed, while other associations in Minnesota, Iowa, Kansas and California formed clubs and held conventions mimicking the National Association's by-laws and playing rules. In 1866, the number of teams belonging to the National Association nearly doubled to 202 teams, and by 1867 almost 350 teams had joined.

A look at the states of origin of the member teams, however, doesn't support the theory of the circulation of the game throughout the entire country by Civil War soldiers—especially in the South. Seventeen states and the District of Columbia were represented at the 1866 meeting of the National Association, most still from New York with 73 clubs, followed by Pennsylvania with 48, and third was New Jersey with 26 teams accounted for at roll call. Other areas of the country sent representatives including Maine, Oregon, Vermont, Missouri and Tennessee. By 1867, it was clear that the spread of the game of baseball hadn't been shaped by Civil War troops moving south during the War but, rather, the Association's records of burgeoning baseball teams reflects veterans and pioneers moving west during and after the four year War.

Membership ledgers for the National Association, by 1867, saw fewer delegates from northern teams such as Pennsylvania and Massachusetts than ever before, while Illinois with 56 delegate teams topped the list at the convention, followed by Ohio with 42 and Wisconsin with 25. New York had 24 teams, as did most other northern states; Connecticut had 22; and Maryland had over 20 teams in attendance. The rest of the states at the Convention represented a small sampling of northern and southern teams.[116]

The overwhelming movement of the game, if quantified by Association records, would detail a growth in the game of baseball that was well on its way before the War interrupted its climb. They would show a resurgence after the Civil War as American populations were moving west, while the decimated South put itself back together again during the long years of Reconstruction. For the half-dozen years following the Civil War, the game of baseball continued to spread dramatically throughout the mid-west and the northeast.[117]

The National Association of Base Ball Players remained in existence for only a few short years following the Civil War. The push towards professionalism in the game was too overwhelming for an Association that wanted the game to remain a social, gentlemanly enterprise. In fact, even during the War years, games and "championship matches" were still played via a formal written invitation by a challenging team. The Association went about its routine business, accepting clubs as members, and excluding clubs "composed of one or more colored persons"—the rule to exclude colored persons was passed in 1867. In 1869, the professionals seized control of the National Association of Base Ball Players.[118]

According to *The Game of Baseball,* published in 1868 and compiled largely from excerpts of the Beadle's baseball guides, a professional player was anyone who played baseball for money or as a means of livelihood.[119] Charging the few professional teams and managers with "lowering the national game to the level of hippodroming of the turf," an article in *The New York Clipper* dated December 18, 1869 (most likely written by Henry Chadwick), feared the "Philistines" would take over the majority of players who preferred the Association to remain a league of amateur teams. The proponents of professionalism succeeded in dividing the amateur and professional clubs so that by 1871 the professionals formed the National Association of Professional Base Ball Players. On March 4 of 1871, representatives of nine clubs met in New York. The Bostons of Boston, the Athletics of Philadelphia, the Atlantics of Brooklyn, the Mutuals of New York, the Haymakers of Troy, the White Stockings of Chicago, the Forest Citys of Rockford, Illinois, the Forest Citys of Cleveland and the Kekiongas of Fort Wayne ended the control of the game by the National Association of Base Ball Players. They made sure that baseball was, from then on—strictly business.[120]

Many historians and writers, during the years following the Civil War, credited the hostilities, *and* the game of baseball, with healing powers that helped solidify the fractionated north and south. In his memoirs, Ulysses S. Grant, for example, penned that the War "begot a spirit of independence and enterprise" and that "There is now such a commingling of the people that particular idioms and pronunciation are no longer localized to any extent...The War has made us a nation of great power and intelligence."[121]

A writer of the 1869 *DeWitt Guide* spoke of the "listlessness and love of indolent pleasures which has too long been a blot on the escutcheon of Southern youths" and endorsed the masculine play of games for the benefit of players and their feminine congregations on both sides of the Mason/Dixon line.

"The late war," they concluded, "proved conclusively their [Southern boys'] powers of physical endurance, as it did the courage, pluck and nerve which they can bring to bear in their efforts to accomplish any task in which their hearts are engaged; and now that peace once more reigns in the land, and that the factionists of both sections of the country are daily giving ground before the advancing steps of a social as well as

44

"CHAMPION NINE" OF THE ATLANTIC BASE-BALL CLUB OF BROOKLYN, L. I., 1865.

Harper's Weekly began to feature players of baseball games in their weekly paper by the end of the Civil War. The "Champion Nine" of the Atlantic Base-Ball Club. November 1865.

Harper's Weekly, The New Jersey State Library.

a political reformation, and manly games and trials of athletic skill have taken the place of the bloody contests on the field of battle, we hope to see the manly qualifications we have alluded to, developed to an extent hitherto unknown in the annals of the South... In fact, what cricket is for the noble dames of England, to grace with their presence, so is base-ball for the patronage of the refined and cultivated classes of the fair belles of America, North and South alike."[122]

The widely distributed periodical, *Harper's Weekly*, also concurred that baseball had benefits that went beyond athletic stimulation. While reporting on the play in New York of the Athletic Base-Ball Club of Philadelphia in June of 1865, the editors commented on the game of baseball as being "most attractive." They concluded that there was "no nobler or manlier game than base-ball, and the more it is cultivated the better for the country." (*Harper's Weekly*, June 17, 1865)

Writers of the 20th century went even further in their pronouncement of the importance of the game of baseball. In a speech titled "Baseball and the American Character" delivered to the Massachusetts Historical Society in October of 1985, A. Bartlett Giamatti discussed the growth of baseball in antebellum America, during the Civil War, through the Reconstruction of the South and through the first World War. He declared to his audience at the Boston Public Library:

> *Baseball grew in the surge of fraternalism, to fraternal societies, sodalities, associations and aggregations, that followed the fratricide. Baseball showed who had won the War and where the country was building, which was in the industrialized North.*[123]

Boys and men who remained home from the War continued to play ball while returning veterans picked up the pieces of their lives—some of them played ball in the north and the south and in the west. Only a few accounts give credit to

45

soldiers for teaching the game to a new generation of young men.

It has often been said that Albert Spalding learned the game as a 13 year-old growing up in Rockford, Illinois, from a Civil War veteran.[124] Spalding himself debunked the legend and only accounted for the fact that he remembered a soldier telling him about baseball played by troops during the War.[125] Many years after the Civil War, B. Chambers of Albuquerque wrote to the *Sporting News*, "My Father was in the Civil War and I used to listen to him tell how they played baseball behind the lines in those trouble days."[126] Perhaps his father taught him the game he played during the War?

In some areas of the north, south and west, townball was still a popular game after the War. It was still played with enthusiasm in front of large crowds in Atlanta, Georgia, in 1866 and 1867 as reported in *The Atlanta Journal* on March 9, 1924. For the most part, however, the New York game of baseball continued to spread just as it did before the War.

Accounts of most veterans do not reveal any direct affiliation with the game of baseball that carried over from the War years. Records of the Grand Army of the Republic (the largest veteran organization for Union soldiers), for example, actually discouraged the playing of games at reunions, encampments and on Memorial Days. They were dismayed when the public spent such solemn occasions as Memorial Day at picnics, fairs, horse races, dances, or at baseball games.[127]

Memorial Day services were a time of reflection and for honoring the dead. Bearded veterans met at the gravesites of their fallen comrades all over the United States to place flowers and American or Confederate flags on the graves. Members of the Batavia Valley Soldiers' Union, as just one example, gathered each Memorial Day as a stipulation of their by-laws. They assembled every year on the "camp ground of

Homer Davenport sketched this image of a Civil War veteran
explaining the game of baseball to a young Albert Spalding. Spalding
denied that the meeting ever took place, although the story lived on
for decades. Ca. 1911. Spalding Collection, Miriam and Ira D. Wallach
Division of Art, Prints and Photographs, The New York Public Library, Astor
Lenox and Tilden Foundations.

the dead, to pay a tribute of love and respect to the memory of our comrades who have joined the ranks of those on the other shore. Year after year, as we perform this sad though grateful duty," they wrote in 1896, "it is with thinned ranks."[128]

Every year following the Civil War, veterans reunited at recruiting places, on old campgrounds, on battlefields and at the sites of former prisons to listen to speeches, meet wives and children, eat lavish banquets and to exchange war stories. There was little time or energy—just as during the War—for games of baseball.

Baseball continued to progress at a rapid pace, however, when the hostilities were over, as the game professionalized to become the favorite of American pastimes. The question of when and how baseball became our "National" game did not come into debate again until the first decade of the 1900s. The mood of the country at the turn of the century linked the War to a strong sense of patriotism, making the connection of a Civil War general and baseball a perfect union.

C hapter 5

That "Asinine Pastime" of Rounders

At the turn of the 20th century, scores of immigrants continued to arrive on American shores. Many Americans believed that these immigrants were the cause of most of the social ills in the United States. A series of immigration laws aimed to deny entry and permit deportation of people with anarchists ideals, placed literacy requirements on would-be immigrants, and made certain that recent arrivals to America were no longer being naturalized for voting purposes.[129]

The growing desire of Americans, with nativist attitudes, to secure a population of citizens in the United States of proper stock and upbringing, coincided with the preoccupation of many Americans with the nation's glorious past.

Following the Civil War, and through the first decades of the 20th century, a "spirit of 'organic nationalism'" prevailed and turned the attention of the population to the founding of the United States and to all the events that contributed to the country's greatness. The centennial celebration of the American Revolution sparked the formation and growth of many patriotic societies such as the Sons and Daughters of the American Revolution, the Society of Colonial Wars and the Colonial Dames. People flocked to libraries at the close of the century to find genealogical ties to their ancestors who fought in the Revolution or who arrived years earlier as pilgrims on the Mayflower.[130] Women's and men's organizations fought to preserve historic homes and worked to create museums—all in an effort to salvage and glorify the country's past. It was during this climate of patriotism and growing xenophobia, that a commission was formed to determine the true and correct origins of the game of baseball.

One man, whose great wealth also financed the commission, spearheaded these efforts. Albert Spalding, founder of A. G. Spalding & Brothers, the firm that supplied the nation with sporting goods, saw baseball as the "exponent of American Courage, Confidence, Combativeness; American Dash, Discipline, Determination; American Energy, Eagerness, Enthusiasm; American Pluck, Persistency, Performance; American Spirit, Success; American Vim, Vigor, and Virility."

Spalding's good friend and editor of his popular baseball guides, Henry Chadwick, an Englishman who grew up in Brooklyn, had for years suggested that the American game of baseball had evolved from the English game of rounders. Spalding was never impressed with the game and insisted that baseball evolved from the American game of one-old-cat, which he concurred later, developed into the game of townball. "Baseball," he lamented, "did not originate from Rounders any more than Cricket originated from that asinine pastime." Native pride and patriotism called for a national game that was devoid of any foreign ancestry.[131]

The debate from any point of view, almost one hundred years later, seems silly. Both games involved batting a ball and running around bases. The shape of the bat, the size of the ball and the shape of the field differed slightly (bats or paddles and balls were smaller in rounders), but both games were simplified games of what we today would recognize as baseball. What makes the debate interesting is that it happened at all. And that the findings of the commission remain part of the nostalgia and patriotic allure of baseball and the reason for the village of Cooperstown becoming the Mecca for the game.

This is one image Albert Spalding used as an illustration to glorify the play of baseball in army camps and in prisons in this patriotic drawing he had made for his early baseball history book. Ca. 1911. Spalding Collection, Miriam and Ira D. Wallach Division of Art, Prints and Photographs, The New York Public Library, Astor Lenox and Tilden Foundations.

A one-time ball player himself, Albert Spalding grew up in a prosperous household in Byron, Illinois, in the 1850s. His father died when he was a young boy and shortly afterwards his mother sent him to the larger city of Rockford to take advantage of the better schools. By his own account, Spalding was an extremely shy boy; "so bashful" he barely went out of the house.[132] Baseball quickly changed all that.

Within a few years, Spalding was described as "statuesque" by baseball reporters, and at 6'2" with a powerful arm, he had made a name for himself in baseball circles as the star pitcher for the Forest City Baseball club. A natural talent, discovered completely by accident, Albert Spalding soon realized athletics, even in 1866, could easily become a priority over his schoolwork. His mother was disturbed to find that the principal of Spalding's high school, Mr. Blodgett, saw fit to excuse Albert from afternoon classes on more than one occasion to play ball.[133]

Spalding worked as a part-time bookkeeper after school and beginning in the spring of 1869, his team, the Forest Citys, beat every club of consequence in Illinois, Indiana, Ohio, St. Louis, Omaha, Nebraska City, along the east coast, and south into New Orleans. Spalding went on to tour with the Forest City Baseball club in the spring of 1870, humiliating most teams in the seventeen game tour except the Athletics of Philadelphia, the Mutuals of Brooklyn and the Chicago White Stockings.[134] Baseball, from then on, became a lifetime passion for Albert Spalding even after his playing days were over.

One paragraph, signed by Spalding in 1905 and published in *Spalding's Official Baseball Guide,* started the work of the seven-man baseball commission to determine *impartially* the origins of the game of baseball:

"What is the origin of BASE BALL? Did it originate from the English Game of
ROUNDERS
The Colonial Game of ONE OLD CAT
The New England and Philadelphia Game of TOWN BALL Or WHAT?"[135]

John Ward's pamphlet, entitled *Baseball, How to Become a Player with the Origin, History, and Explanation of the Game* criticized unpatriotic "persons who believed that everything good and beautiful in the world must be of English origin."[136] People like Spalding and his cohort A. G. Mills liked what they read in the monograph, and for years it served as unofficial proof that baseball was unequivocally an American game. Why Albert Spalding went on the quest to prove baseball was 100% American, even to the point of fanaticism, is not totally understood, although it did help in the mass marketing of his products. We do know that baseball, as he often admitted, was Spalding's "first and last love."[137]

Spalding was a powerful figure in baseball and business circles and his requests to sit on the commission to determine the origins of baseball were not to be denied. In fact, he handpicked all the committee members including two United States senators. James E. Sullivan of New York, president of the Amateur Athletic Union, accepted the position of secretary of the special Baseball Commission called for by Spalding. Abraham G. Mills, third president of the National League, was named chairman. Mills was also an old-time ball player, Civil War Veteran and GAR post member with Civil War General Abner Doubleday. He wanted it distinctly understood that "patriotism and research" had proven baseball to be solely American in origin.[138]

Over the next two and a half years, the committee conducted interviews and gathered evidence concerning the

Albert Spalding. Spaulding Collection, Miriam and Ira D. Wallach Division of Art, Prints and Photographs, The New York Public Library, Astor Lenox and Tilden Foundations.

true root of the game. Secretary Sullivan wrote in 1908 that he was "deluged with communications from different parts of the country" concerning the question of baseball's true beginnings.[139] Unfortunately, few of these communications survive. A fire destroyed the records housed in the offices of the American Sports Publishing Company, where Sullivan worked, and only a few pieces of the evidence gathered are known to exist. Two letters ended up with correspondence kept by A. G. Mills.[140] One letter was written by Philip W. Hudson of Houston, Texas. He wrote to the Commission in July of 1905:

> *I am a native of hartford, Conn., and have, from early boyhood, taken a great interest in all Out Door Sports that are clean and manly. As a boy I played One, Two, Three and Four Old Cat; also the old time game of "Wicket." I remember that before the Civil War, I don't now remember how long, we played base ball at my home, Manchester, Hartford Co., Ct. When the war came on I went to the front in April, a member of the 1st Ct. Regt. In the Winter of 1863 we were sent to St. Helena Island, and while there the officers of the 24th Mass. (All young gentlemen from Boston), got up a base ball club and we played base ball often. I played with them. We had many clubs in Connecticut and I was President of one in Manchester, and also played with them.*
>
> *I am confident that Base Ball is strictly an American game. There were no English players in our town, but I had more or less Englishmen in New York employ who when seeing us play Base Ball would always say: "Why don't you men play cricket—that's the game."[141]*

This letter was entered as an exhibit for the American side of the argument (exhibit numbered 57-25) and is most likely

53

typical of the kind of material gathered by the special Commission. The only other letter known to this author sounds remarkably similar in its tone. William Cauldwell stated in February of 1905:

> *As an old attache of the New York Sunday Mercury, with which I was identified forty-five years, I take pleasure in responding to your inquiry concerning the history of Base Ball, in which you manifest so deep an interest.*
>
> *I may say that I can speak as a New York boy from away back, and in all my experience I had no knowledge of the prominence of a ball game named "Rounders." I played ball in my native city from the time when I was (to use an old time phrase) "knee high to a mosquito," dated back to when 14th st. was considered out of town, and I can speak from what I know...* [142]

The evidence was hardly compelling enough to support any theory. But the most unsubstantiated letter, published in 1905 before the fire at the offices of Sullivan, was written by an elderly mining engineer, who in his late years, murdered his wife and ended up in an asylum for the criminally insane where he died in 1926. It was used by the Commission to rest its case on the origin of baseball.

Abner Graves of Cooperstown and Denver, Colorado, wrote to the Baseball Commission in April of 1905:

> *The American game of Base Ball was invented by Abner Doubleday, of Cooperstown, N.Y., either the Spring prior, or following the "Log Cabin and Hard Cider" campaign of General Harrison for President, said Abner Doubleday being then a boy pupil of "Green's Select School" in Cooperstown, and the same who as General*

Doubleday won honor at the battle of Gettysburg in the Civil War...[143]

Graves described the games of townball that were played on the grassy fields of the Otsego Campus and at the old Phinney Farm along the west shore of Lake Otsego in Cooperstown. His childhood playmate, Doubleday, as he remembered, figured out and made a plan to improve townball by limiting the number of players, by having equal sides, and by using three bases for the runners to round before reaching home in a diamond-shaped playing field. Doubleday called the game "Base Ball" because it had four bases. And its "invention" Graves wrote, was entitled to Abner Doubleday and "is undoubtedly a pure American game."[144]

The problems with Grave's recollections are many and have been well documented. We do know that Doubleday was a cadet at West Point in 1839, the year that baseball was supposedly invented. In fact, his entire family had left Cooperstown two years earlier. Graves was born in Cooperstown in 1834 and Doubleday was born in Ballston Spa in 1819, making him 15 years older than Graves. If Graves's memory was correct, his childhood playmate was 20 and he was but 5 years old. Another Abner Doubleday, a cousin of the General, was living in Cooperstown at the right time to have been the Doubleday that Graves remembered. This Abner was born in 1823. Little is known of him except for a listing in the 1893 *Biographical Review of Otsego County*.[145]

No published works about the game of baseball and Abner Doubleday were written before the baseball commission began its tedious work. Doubleday himself wrote several articles for publication and kept 67 diaries throughout his life that not once mention baseball. Even his obituary of 1893 fails to mention his connection to the game. One letter exists that speaks of baseball and was written by Doubleday after the

Civil War while he served as Colonel of the 24th U.S. Colored Infantry stationed in Fort McKavett, Texas.

He wrote to General E. D. Townsend in 1871 asking for supplies:

General:

I have the honor to apply for permission to purchase for the Regimental Library a few portraits of distinguished generals, Battle pictures, and some of Rogers groups of Statuary particularly those relative to the actions of the Colored population of the south.

This being a Colored regiment ornaments of this kind seem very appropriate. I would also like to purchase baseball implements for the amusement of the men and a magic lantern for the same purpose. The fund is ample and I think these expenditures would add to the happiness of the men....[146]

Doubleday was well respected and liked by his men and it appears, like many commanders, he understood the importance of leisure-time activities, including baseball, for the morale of his men. As the only known written document that links Doubleday to baseball, it is appreciated but does not conclude any connection to the "invention" of the game. Abner Doubleday's greatest distinction will remain his heroic actions on the fields of Gettysburg, Pennsylvania.

In the summer of 1863, General Robert E. Lee, the Confederate commander of forces in the east, convinced President Davis to approve a bold plan. He was again prepared to take a major offensive against the north. Lee marched his army northward from Richmond into enemy territory, horrifying civilians and the Union army, who followed in pursuit from Maryland. The two armies clashed by accident in the little town of Gettysburg and Abner Doubleday was there.

Major General Abner Doubleday. An obituary written by a classmate from West Point eulogized Doubleday as being "A man who did not care for or go to any outdoor sports." Massachusetts Commandery, Military Order of the Loyal Legion and the US Army Military History Institute.

The Union army was under the command of the newly appointed George Gordon Meade. On the first day of fighting on July 1, 1863, Federal Major General John Reynolds and his 1st Corps arrived to find the two armies already immovably engaged. As he began to ready his troops, a Confederate sharpshooter killed Reynolds instantly with a bullet behind the ear. Abner Doubleday bravely took over command of his troops—against heavy odds—holding the Confederate forces at bay until the first day's fighting was over. His division was also in the thick of the fighting on the second and third days of combat (July 2 and July 3, 1863), and assisted in successfully defending the middle of Meade's defensive line against Pickett's famous charge across the three-quarter-mile-wide field between Seminary and Cemetery ridges.

Doubleday remained bitterly offended for the rest of his life after being passed over for the permanent command of the Corps by General Meade, following the fall of General Reynolds. Meade gave the assignment to an old classmate of Doubleday from West Point named Newton. Gettysburg was the last time Doubleday commanded soldiers in the field. He went on duty in Washington until the close of the War. (*The Dictionary of American Biography*)

Some historians have credited Abner Doubleday with firing the first shot by the Union army at the start of the Civil War. Stationed in Charleston Harbor, South Carolina, in 1860-61, Doubleday was second in command at Fort Sumter in the spring of 1861. President Lincoln had refused to abandon the fort to the Confederate government, even as war seemed imminent. Doubleday wrote in a book of his reminiscences that it was he who fired the first shot in defense of the fort in response to the Confederate bombardment on April 12, 1861. Doubleday recalled:

> *As I was the ranking officer, I took the first detachment and marched them to the casements which looked out upon the powerful ironclad battery of Cummings Point.*
>
> *In aiming the first gun fired against the rebellion I had no feeling of self-reproach, for I fully believe that the contest was inevitable and was not of our seeking...[147]*

Supposedly, the shot bounded off the sloping roof of an ironclad ship in the harbor without producing any apparent ill effect. The Union Army eventually surrendered the fort after 35 hours of heavy shelling by the Confederate army under the command of General Beauregard. The Union Army left the outpost on April 14, 1861.

Doubleday went on to develop a distinguished career, rising to the rank of major general before retiring from military life in December of 1873. He was a perfect patriotic candidate to become the inventor of America's national game and Albert Spalding knew it.

"It certainly appeals to an American's pride," wrote Spalding, "to have had the great national game of Base Ball created and named by a Major General in the United States Army and to have that same game played as a camp diversion by the soldiers of the Civil War...[148] "It is fascinating to wonder what the other generals would have said," wrote historian Bruce Catton, in a retrospect on Doubleday's career, "if they could have known that in the end Doubleday was going to be one of the most famous of them all—not for his war record, but for his alleged connection with the origin of the game of baseball...[149]

And so the baseball commission made a determination that was unanimously accepted by all the members after months of sorting through the "mass of evidence" collected. The task

The 76th Regiment New York State Volunteers were situated in defense of Washington, D.C. for a time during the Civil War, where Abner Doubleday had a camp named for him. This view appeared on the stationary of Lieutenant Colonel John Shaul and in the 1866 history of the 76th regiment written by A. P. Smith. It has been reproduced on T-shirts and commemorative envelopes in defense of the "Doubleday myth." A closer look reveals that two soldiers are batting a ball with bats or paddles, not playing a game of baseball. The New York State Library.

force concluded just in time to publish the decision in *Spalding's Official Base Ball Guide* in 1908:

"Baseball," they wrote, "is of American origin, and has no traceable connection whatever with 'Rounders,' or any other foreign game."[150]

The committee also resolved that a Civil War general named Abner Doubleday was the inventor of the game. Americans had found a "glorious" national game that was in everyway "suited to the American Character."[151] It wasn't until the coming of the Centennial Celebration of the birth of baseball, that the findings of the commission came into full-fledged scrutiny.

The United States Postal Service featured this "All-American" scene on the postage stamp in honor of the Centennial of Baseball in 1839. The Postal Service admitted that the celebration in Cooperstown that year was founded on "questionable premises" but accepted the date of 1839 as the official centennial year. National Baseball Hall of Fame Library and Archive, Cooperstown, NY.

C hapter 6

One Hundred Years of Baseball

At the opening ceremonies of the celebration of one hundred years of baseball in Cooperstown, New York, the Honorable Bert Lord of the 34th Congressional district presented a baseball to the "National Baseball Museum" that was pitched at the opening of the baseball season in April of 1939. He congratulated the tiny village of Cooperstown on having such a wonderful baseball diamond made in honor of Abner Doubleday. He also commented on how proud he was to have been part of the ceremonies some years before, when a statue to the same Abner Doubleday was unveiled on the battlefield at Gettysburg. It was a beautiful spring day on May 6, 1939, and 3,500 people turned out to see the "first baseball diamond" marked out by Abner Doubleday on the old Phinney pasture on the western end of the village of Cooperstown.[152]

The planning for the summer-long festivities began on June 1, 1937, when representatives of several village civic groups met in the Village Hall to develop a permanent organization to format plans for the Centennial Celebration of Baseball. Mayor Theodore Lettis of Cooperstown was named chairman. By January of 1939, the organization had formed a corporation and announced that it would finance the Centennial through the sale of loan certificates to local businesses and residents.

The work began quickly in February to restore the "historic" Doubleday field and to erect temporary and permanent bleachers to seat a capacity crowd of 10,000.

Thirty-four workers from the Federal Works Administration were expected to complete the work by the spring for the first of the scheduled events. It was an exciting time in the village. Even the majority of Cooperstown residents, who were normally opposed to daylight savings time, voted 532 to 152 to impose the "fast" time from April 30 through September 24 during the peak of the Baseball Centennial.[153]

Years before the Centennial Commission was formed, a small discovery in 1935 sparked the interest of a local philanthropist and created the impetus for an even larger Centennial celebration in Cooperstown. A farmer, and relative of Abner Graves (the man whose testimony was used to determine the origins of the game), found an old baseball in a trunk in the attic of his house in Fly Creek, a small hamlet outside of the village of Cooperstown. It was purchased for the National Baseball Museum in Cooperstown, then housed in the Village Club building.[154] This old, worn baseball was put on exhibit and soon came to be known as the "Abner Doubleday baseball." It seemed logical enough at the time, that if the ball was found in Graves's attic and dated to around the time baseball was "invented," then it must have been handled by Doubleday.

The local philanthropist was Stephen C. Clark, an heir to the Singer sewing machine fortune. Clark money had built much of Cooperstown including a hotel, a hospital, a gymnasium and an 18-hole golf course. Stephen was also a noted patron of the New York State Historical Association headquartered in the village. Until the discovery of the "Doubleday ball," Clark had shown little or no interest in baseball. He understood, however, that tourism was the only way to boost the economy in an area where farming used to sustain many of the villagers.

Clark's $5.00 purchase of the baseball inspired plans for an all-out baseball museum. His foundation put up the $43,000

BASE-BALL.

An early illustration of what appears to be Civil War soldiers playing baseball appeared in a rule book of games, *The American Boy's Book of Sports and Games* in 1864. Reprint, Author's Collection.

to build the museum on the land that he had donated. He and his colleagues had no problem convincing major league baseball dignitaries to sanction his plans—especially during the Depression when baseball attendance was dwindling.[155] On December 8, 1937, the National and American Leagues voted to approve $100,000 to help finance the Centennial Celebrations in Cooperstown.[156] All was going well with the Museum and the plans for the Centennial, until a reputable historian published an article called "Baseball and Rounders" and a disturbing letter arrived from a descendant of Alexander Cartwright, of the late Knickerbocker Club of New York, to baseball commissioner Kenesaw Landis.

Robert W. Henderson published an article in April of 1939 in the _Bulletin of the New York Public Library_ entitled "Baseball and Rounders." Inspired by a small edition of the 19th century book _Boys and Girls Book of Sports_ donated to the library by Miss Beatrice Gunn earlier that year, Henderson was motivated to explore the "long dormant controversy" between the two theories on the development of the game of baseball.

The little book published in 1836, three years before Doubleday supposedly devised the game, printed rules for "the great American game." Investigations of even earlier editions of other children's books of games and sports chronicled rules and drawings for the game of baseball. Henderson methodically detailed the history of the game back to the 18th century in America. He was the first author to debunk the Doubleday myth in a documented article, which included supportive evidence that noted Doubleday's absence in Cooperstown in 1839 and refuted the testimony of an elderly Graves. Famous author Will Irwin had challenged the Doubleday stories in a series of articles written for _Collier's Weekly_ in 1909, but he did not provide any specifics to substantiate his theory.[157]

63

Henderson also made the first connection between Doubleday and A. G. Mills, a Civil War comrade. It was Mills who made the arrangements for Doubleday's funeral and for his body to lay in state at the New York City Hall. His death announcement in the *New York Times*, dated January 29, 1893, called the members of the Grand Army of the Republic Lafayette post number 140 to assemble at the railway station in Hoboken, New Jersey, on the following Monday to escort the body of the late Abner Doubleday. Mills, as post commander, called on his fellow veterans to report in full uniform with proper caps and white gloves for the funeral procession. Doubleday's body was later escorted to Washington for burial. (*New York Times*, January 29, 1893)

Neither Doubleday's obituary nor the memorial volumes published by the New York State Monuments Commission in 1918 mention Doubleday with any connection to baseball. The honor was given to him in 1906 when the first press release connecting him to baseball was released by the Baseball Commission under the guidance of A. G. Mills.[158]

Not only did the article by Henderson call into doubt whether or not a commemorative celebration and new ball park should be erected in Cooperstown, but a letter written by Bruce Cartwright, grandson to Alexander Cartwright, pointed out to the Baseball Commissioner that there was a serious omission in credits due. Bruce Cartwright had written proof of the rules for the "modern" game of baseball drafted in 1845 by Alexander and the Knickerbocker Club. These rules called for nine men to a team, flat bases, three outs per team and the key to the New York game—a diamond-shaped played field with bases ninety feet apart.[159]

As a surveyor, Cartwright is credited with figuring the perfect distance to challenge a cleanly handled grounder thrown to first base matched against the speed of a runner. Of all the rule changes over the years, this 90-foot distance remains the same.[160] For his contribution to the game of baseball, a plaque rests on the grounds of the Elysian Fields in Hoboken, New Jersey. It marks the spot where the first widely recognized match game was played under the Knickerbocker rules between the Knickerbockers and the New York Club on June 19, 1846.

The New York Club had been playing on Elysian Fields for several years before the famous game against the Knicks. They celebrated their second anniversary on the field in 1845, having met there regularly since 1843.[166]

Unfortunately, Bruce Cartwright's efforts did not result in a full tribute to his grandfather. He died a few weeks after the letter was delivered to Commissioner Landis. It is not known how many others knew of its contents. To cover themselves, the Baseball Centennial Committee quickly added an "Alexander Cartwright Day" to the Centennial program[161] and the celebrations went off without a hitch.

After the tablet was affixed to the grandstand entrance announcing Doubleday Field as the "Birthplace of Baseball," the crowd stood as the cadets played "The Star Spangled Banner." "The cadet battalions at attention, the blue sky in which a few scattered clouds lazily floated, the pennant-topped bleachers and the historic field all presented a picture that will never be forgotten by any who were present," as described by the staff of the *Freeman's Journal* of Cooperstown in 1940.[162] A few weeks later the celebrations continued as the new National Baseball Hall of Fame and Museum opened on June 12, 1939, to an unprecedented crowd of twelve thousand. The first 25 ball players were inducted into the Hall—among them were the legendaries Babe Ruth and Cy Young.[163]

From that point on, there was no turning back for Cooperstown. Doubleday became a forgotten Civil War hero, replaced by a baseball legend. Even as a few sports columnists made note of the discrepancy at the time of the Centennial, too many people—even the State of New York— had bought into the Doubleday invention and advertised the birthplace of baseball in Conservation Department brochures and on road signs erected for the 100 year anniversary.[164] It wasn't long before The National Baseball Hall of Fame and Museum became a pilgrimage stop for hundreds of thousands of people a year. Most people, unknowingly, accept Cooperstown as the hallowed ground of baseball. It looks the ideal spot—a rural town still looking like a nostalgic postcard from the 19th century and far away from the city sprawl of Hoboken, New Jersey.

One Hundred Years Of Baseball

One hundred years of Baseball,
Turn back historic pages;
The game that's now a century old
Has flourished through the ages.

A hundred years of wholesome sport,
Replete with skill and action;
A game that knows no boundary lines
Of race or creed or faction.

A game that's thrilled the rich and poor
The mighty and the humble;
Each knows the joy of sparkling play,
The tragedy of fumble.

The melting pot of human souls,
Where elbows rub together;
Where banker cheers with tradesman
At the crash of bat and leather.

One hundred years of Baseball!
May it thrive a thousand more;
May it show a winning record
When posterity asks the score.

L. H. Addington

Dedicated at the celebrations of the
100th anniversary of baseball.[165]

Men lay down their bats and balls to volunteer in defense of their country during the Civil War. Ca. 1911. Spalding Collection, Spalding Collection, Miriam and Ira D. Wallach Division of Art, Prints and Photographs, The New York Public Library, Astor Lenox and Tilden Foundations.

The Civil War: A Brief History

The events leading up to the Civil War had been brewing since the colonies were settled. The question of whether slavery should be permitted in each new territory of the growing country was a recurrent and hotly debated issue since the forming of the United States in 1787. Even in the Constitution, the framers elected to compromise on the issue of slavery and forbade the interference with foreign slave trade until 1808. States' rights—the belief by many southerners that the new Union was formed by sovereign states that retained the right to withdraw from the union—motivated the secession of South Carolina in December of 1860. Ten other states, also believing in state sovereignty, followed South Carolina to form the Confederate States of America.

The population of the South at the time was about 9 million people. Almost 4 million of these people were slaves. The North would clearly have the advantage in any conflict, with a population of 19 million people, a thriving railroad system and industrialized cities manufacturing every conceivable kind of product. In the 1860s, the South's predominant industry was still agriculture and cotton, a leading export, that relied upon a work force of slaves to plant, cultivate and harvest the crop.

Union soldiers refused to abandon the Federal fort of defense at Fort Sumter in Charleston Harbor, South Carolina (then in the territory of the newly formed Confederacy). Subsequently, the War began on April 12, 1861, with the bombardment of the fort by Confederate guns. The Federal Army left in defeat and within a few days President Lincoln called for volunteers to enlist in defense of the Union. The newly elected President of the Confederacy, Jefferson Davis, asked the same of his countrymen, calling recruits into military service in defense of the Confederate States of America.

Very few people in the divided country thought the War would be a long one. Only one famous general, William Tecumseh Sherman, predicted a prolonged and costly fight. Most new recruits who joined the cause, whether for the north or the south, had little experience, if any, in the ways of the military. Many were also unsure of their desire to defend a severed country or a newly formed republic or to free an enslaved people. It wasn't until the reading of the Emancipation Proclamation by Abraham Lincoln after the Battle of Antietam in September of 1863, that the War truly became a war to end slavery in the minds of most Americans.

A series of Union defeats and embarrassments followed the loss of Fort Sumter, including the first Battle of Bull Run in 1861 where the Federal Army listed over 2,900 casualties and the American public woke up to the reality and the horror of the War. Battles were fought in the western theaters of Kentucky and Mississippi and Tennessee, and in the east, especially in Virginia, as the armies sought to protect the two capitals of the warring governments. Washington, D.C., and Richmond, Virginia, rested barely 100 miles apart. Only twice did the Confederate Army make advances into Union boundaries, one time along Antietam Creek in Maryland in 1862 and once at Gettysburg, Pennsylvania, in the summer of 1863.

The Federal Army went through generals quickly— McClellan, Burnside, Hooker and Meade—as Lincoln looked for the right leader to end the War. General Ulysses S. Grant, who had gained a reputation as a fighter in the west, was finally given command of the entire Union Army in 1864 against a formidable foe from Virginia, General Robert E. Lee. Their two armies would face each other several times in places like the Wilderness, Cold Harbor and Spotsylvania.

70

Back home, northern industries were booming as wartime demands kept factories humming. In the southern states, the Confederacy struggled to keep its people fed, its army clothed, and gold in reserves to back the deflated paper money floating between the government, civilians and enlisted men. The blockade of southern ports by the Federal navy compounded the problems of shrinking resources in the south. Though the north fared better financially during the vulnerable war years, both sides became quickly disillusioned with the War as casualty numbers soared. Most soldiers fell victim to disease, not combat wounds, and thousands suffered and died of starvation in prison camps, especially towards the end of the War when both armies stopped exchanging prisoners who often turned into new recruits to reinforce the ranks. In the end, the War would claim over half a million men.

Lee and Grant faced each other for the last time at Appomattox Court House, Virginia, when Lee surrendered the last of the thinning Confederate lines to Grant on April 9 of 1865, after the fall of Petersburg and Richmond, Virginia. The War of attrition had finally worn a proud army into submission. It would take years to reunite the two factions of the country—many fear both have never truly forgotten nor forgiven.

One thing all Americans always had, and still have, in common, despite the geography of their home, is the love of sport. During the decades leading to the Civil War, leisure-time activities were thriving. It became socially acceptable to exercise and take part in sport either as a competitor or as a fan. The sport industry was taking off. Ice skating on New York's Central Park pond was all the rage, and bicycle riding, tennis, lawn croquet, ocean bathing and a long list of other outdoor amusements were encouraged for the health and well-being of participants. Americans joined athletic clubs, read about sport in newspapers and magazines, and saw images of games in published lithographs and photographs. By the onset of the Civil War, the game of baseball had become a developing business waiting for the return of hundreds of thousands of men to take part in the game at the close of the War.

Baseball: *A Chronology of Baseball in England and America Leading up to the Civil War (1621-1860)*

1621- Governor Bradford was disturbed by boys playing "stoole ball" and other sports at Plymouth Colony in Massachusetts on Christmas Day.

1700- One of the earliest references to baseball, clergyman of Maidstone, England complained of boys playing "Base Ball" on the Sabbath.

1744- A book published in London, *A Little Pretty Pocket Book*, contains the first picture of baseball along with a description of the game.

1748- A letter describes the activities of Frederick, Prince of Wales and his family, "...diverting themselves with baseball, a play all who are or have been schoolboys are well acquainted with."

1762- *A Little Pretty Pocket Book* is published in New York.

1778- George Ewing writes in his diary of playing "Base" at Valley Forge, Pennsylvania, during the Revolutionary War.

1786-1787- "Baste Ball" is played on campus of Princeton University until the faculty objects to the game "...on account of its being dangerous as well as beneath the propriety of a gentleman."

1797- In a letter, Daniel Webster writes of "playing ball" with a student at Dartmouth College.

1798- In her novel entitled, *Northanger Abbey*, Jane Austen writes briefly of "base-ball."

1800- Several books have been printed in the United States and in England describing many versions of bat and ball games called by different names—Base Ball, Rounders, Goal Ball, Feeder, Round Ball—all basically the same.

1816- "Ball-playing" outlawed in the streets of Worcester, Massachusetts.

1820- In a book in New England entitled, *Children's Amusements*, a woodcut appears illustrating boys playing with a bat and ball.

1820's- In Philadelphia, a group of ball players, the forerunners of the Olympic Town Ball Club, organize. Ordinances dating to Puritan times still prohibit the play of ball within city limits.

1825- A well-known journalist and politician, Thurlow Weed, tells of playing base-ball as a young man in the Rochester area—"A base-ball club, numbering nearly fifty members, met every afternoon during the playing season."

1825- On July 13, 1825, the following notice appeared in the Delhi, (N.Y.) *Gazette*, "The undersigned, all residents

74

of the new town of Hamden, with the exception of Asa C. Howland, who has recently removed into Delhi, challenge an equal number of persons of any town in the County of Delaware, to meet them at any time at the house of Edward B. Chace, in said town, to play the game BASS-BALL, for the sum of one dollar each per game. If no town can be found that will produce the required number, they have no objection to play against any selection that can be made from several towns in the county."

1827- William Latham, a student at Brown University wrote in his diary of ball play.

1830- Town Ball, or Americanized Rounders, was popular in New England.

1830- The book, *Children's Amusements*, published in Oxford and New York, illustrates ball playing and makes the following reference: "Playing ball is much practiced by school boys and is an excellent exercise to unbend the mind, and restore to the body that elasticity and spring..."

1831- The Olympic Town Ball Club crosses over to Camden from Philadelphia to play ball away from prohibitive city ordinances.

1834-1835- *The Book of Sport*, published in the United States, contains a set of rules and a diagram of a baseball diamond along with a picture of a "Base Ball" game on Boston Common.

1838- In his novel, *Home As Found*, James Fenimore Cooper describes boys playing ball on the lawn of the home of the Effingham family. The event may have been based on a true-life occurrence in Cooper's life in 1834.

1839- Abner Doubleday supposedly "invented" baseball in Cooperstown, New York. This myth was formulated by a nationalistic commission, to determine the origins of the game. Almost from the beginning, historians discredit the claim although it remains part of American folklore to this day.

1840- In New York City, D. L. Adams played a game that he understood to be baseball—"...with a number of other medical men. Before that there had been a club called the New York Base Ball Club, but it had no very definite organization and did not last long."

1840- Henry Chadwick, noted baseball writer, declared the... "New York Game originated in 1840."

1843- The New York Club played intra-mural games at Elysian Fields in Hoboken, New Jersey.

1845- Alexander Cartwright of the Knickerbocker Baseball Club of New York City fabricates the rules of play for the "modern" game of baseball: bases ninety feet apart, nine men per team, prohibition of "soaking" or hitting a player with the ball and three men out, all out. The Knicks were in the beginning stages of organization as early as 1842.

1845- On Elysian Fields in Hoboken, New Jersey, an inter-club match between the New York Ball Club and a team of Brooklyn players was reported in the *New York Morning News*. New York won - 24 to 4.

1846- What is often cited as the first formal ball game between two organized teams was played on June 19 between the Knickerbockers and New York. Although not the first, this game is used as the starting point of organized play. The Knickerbockers lost the contest - 23 to 1. The game was played under the 1845 regulations.

1849- The Knickerbocker ball club adopts a uniform—blue pants and white polo shirts.

1850s- The game continues to commercialize as many clubs spring up around the New York area. With the rules of the New York game calling for foul lines, spectators can safely become fans away from fair play.

1856- The New York game moves westward to Chicago and all the way to California.

1857- The National Association of Baseball Players is formed as the first amateur baseball association to monitor the game. One of the first rule adoptions was the nine-inning game, ending the old 21 run rule to declare a winner.

1859- The first intercollegiate contest is played between Amherst and Williams Colleges.

1861- The Civil War begins.

**Adapted from the compilations of the "Thumbnail History of Baseball" by John Durant in his book entitled *The Story of*

Baseball in words and pictures, page 274, and from the "Early Baseball Chronology" compiled by the Leatherstocking Base Ball Club of Cooperstown, New York, from the collection of Tom Heitz.

Notes

1. Spalding 1991, 64.
2. Weaver 1939, 98.
3. Smith 1947, 46-47.
4. Prentice Hall, 1990, 109.
5. Hakim 1994, 81.
6. Spalding 1991, 64.
7. Zoss and Bowman 1996, 80.
8. Seymour 1990, 219.
9. Rolfe 1864.
10. Durant and Bettmann 1952, 36 and Henderson 1947, 146.
11. Durant and Bettmann 1952, 6.
12. Hawke 1988, 96.
13. Hawley 1753, 1041.
14. Dulles 1965, 33 and McClintock 1961, 20.
15. Gilbert 1995, 38.
16. Dulles 1965, 33.
17. Goldstein 1989, 10 and Henderson 1947, 146.
18. *Harper's Weekly* October 15 and November 5, 1859.
19. McDonald 1988, 1.
20. Fink 1961, 28-37.
21. Fink 1961, 29.
22. Fink 1961, 35.
23. *Ibid*
24. Kirsch 1989, 3.
25. Seymour 1960, 40.
26. Thomas 1979, 6-8.
27. Wiggins 1979, 68-87.
28. Wiggins 1979, 67.
29. Wiggins 1979, 67-68.

30. Seymour 1990, 291 and Henderson 1947, 136.
31. Cumming 1981, preface.
32. Henderson 1947, 136.
33. Voigt 1966, xxv.
34. Henderson 1947, 147.
35. Durant 1947, 10.
36. Sullivan 1995, 32-33.
37. Spivey 1985, 198.
38. Seymour 1960, 14.
39. Voigt 1996, xxvii.
40. Braden 1988, 199.
41. Voigt 1966, 7-8.
42. "Baseball club...", Newsclipping, September 15, 1985.
43. Ward and Burns 1994, 12.
44. Kirsch 1989, 54 and *Wilke's Spirit of the Times*, December 1, 1860.
45. Malloy 1999.
46. Sullivan 1995, 34-36.
47. Kirsch 1989, 62.
48. Braden 1988, 203.
49. Voigt 1966, 27.
50. Braden 1988, 204.
51. Betts 1971, 115-116 and *New York Clipper*, July 18, 1863.
52. Mills 1923 and Spalding 1991, 68.
53. Beaudry 1996, 114 and Sutherland 1989, 5-6.
54. Seymour 1960, 41.
55. Alstyne 1910, 233.
56. Kaminsky 1997, 26.
57. Crockett 1961, 339.
58. Crockett 1961, 345.
59. Fielding 1977, 5.
60. Wiley 1960, 170.
61. Fielding 1977, 6.

62. Wiley 1960, 64.
63. *Wilke's Spirit of the Times*, February 16, 1861 and Zoss and Bowman 1996, 83.
64. Fielding 1978, 11.
65. Fielding 1978, 16-17.
66. Chisolm 1864, 56-57.
67. Cumming 1981, 63 and Wiley 1960, 174.
68. Fielding 1977, 155.
69. *Ibid.*
70. Kirsch 1989, 79.
71. Betts 1971, 127.
72. Kirsch 1989, 83 and *New York Clipper*, May 21, 1864.
73. Fielding 1977, 8.
74. Harding 1863.
75. Wiley 1960, 159.
76. Crockett 1961, 341.
77. Crockett 1961, 345.
78. Crockett 1961, 342.
79. Fielding 1978, 17-18.
80. Daniel 1960, 14.
81. Sullivan 1995, xvi, 43.
82. Voigt 1966, 10.
83. Mills 1923.
84. Mitchell 1988, 37.
85. Fielding 1977, 160 and Kirsch 1989, 81.
86. Spalding 1991, 65.
87. Twombly 1976, 71.
88. Fielding 1977, 8.
89. Cumming 1981, 63.
90. *New York Clipper*, December 28, 1861 and Rawlings 1998, 48.
91. Wiley 1960, 170 and Wright 1996, 52.
92. Hanifen 1905, 45 and *New York Clipper*, May 14, 1864.

93. Glazier 1866, 303-304.
94. Brown 1980, 16, 34.
95. Applewood Books 1988, 97.
96. Sumner 1997, 51.
97. Sumner 1989, 20.
98. *Ibid.*
99. Sumner 1989, 21.
100. Twombly 1976, 71.
101. *Ibid.*
102. Sumner 1989, 22.
103. Brown 1980, 96.
104. Brown 1980, 104.
105. Brown 1980, 156.
106. Mark Rucker, phone interview September 17, 1998.
107. Kirsch 1989, 80.
108. "The Game Endures..." 1994, 18.
109. *Ibid.*
110. Seymour 1960, 43.
111. Seymour 1960, 41, 43.
112. Voigt 1966, 11-12.
113. Seymour 1960, 37.
114. Voigt 1966, 8-10.
115. Wittke 1939, 1.
116. Merrifield, 20-21 and Seymour 1960, 43-46.
117. Goldstein 1989, 4-5.
118. Sullivan 1995, 68, 77.
119. Sullivan 1995, 71.
120. Bartlett 1951, 39 and Sullivan 1995, 77-78.
121. Grant 1995, 462.
122. Abrams 1994, 72.
123. Giamatti 1985, 5.
124. Merrifield, 20.
125. Bartlett 1951, 24.
126. Seymour 1990, 291.

127. Davies 1955, 217.
128. Batavia Valley Soldier's Union 1896, 5.
129. Millen 1997, 1-4.
130. Davies 1955, 44-47.
131. Bartlett 1951, 2-3 and Spalding 1908, 3.
132. Bartlett 1951, 22-25.
133. Bartlett 1951, 28, 37.
134. Bartlett 1951, 34-35.
135. Alvarez 1990, 30.
136. Alvarez 1990, 28.
137. Bartlett 1951, 2.
138. Seymour 1960, 9.
139. Spalding 1908, 35.
140. Bartlett 1951, 7.
141. Hudson 1905.
142. Cauldwell 1905.
143. Mills papers 1905.
144. Mills papers 1905.
145. *Biographical Review* 1893, Salvatore 1983, 50-52.
146. Thomas 1989.
147. Commager 1960, 35.
148. Alvarez 1990, 34.
149. Twombly 1976, 70.
150. Spalding 1908, 36.
151. Bartlett 1951, 11.
152. *Freeman's Journal* 1940, 21-24.
153. Cooper 1976, 253-259.
154. Cooper 1976, 244.
155. Salvatore 1983, 53-54.
156. Cooper 1976, 255.
157. Henderson 1939, 303-309.
158. Henderson, 1939, 309.
159. Durant and Bettmann 1952, 39.
160. Durant and Bettmann 1952, 41.

161. Salvatore 1983, 55.
162. *Freeman's Journal* 1940, 22.
163. Cooper 1976, 261.
164. Seymour 1960, 11.
165. *Freeman's Journal* 1940, 3.
166. Adelman 1986, 122.

Sources Cited:

Abrams, Joseph Wallace. "The Baseball Anthology."
Cooperstown, NY: exhibit at the National Baseball Hall of
Fame Library. 1994.

Adelman, Melvin L. *A Sporting Time: New York City and the
Rise of Modern Athletics, 1820-1870.* Urbana: University
of Illinois Press. 1986.

Alstyne, Lawrence Van. *Diary of An Enlisted Man.*
Connecticut: The Tuttle, Morehouse and Taylor Company.
1910.

Alvarez, Mark. *The Old Ball Game.* Virginia: Redefinition
Inc. 1990.

An Album of Civil War Battle Art. Cambridge: Applewood
Books. 1988.

Bartlett, Arthur. *Baseball and Mr. Spalding.* New York:
Farrar, Straus and Young. 1951.

"Baseball club formed in Augusta in 1859," newspaper
clipping (title of paper unknown). Cooperstown, NY:
exhibit at the National Baseball Hall of Fame and Library.
15 September 1985.

Batavia Valley Soldier's Union. By-laws. Prattsville, NY:
Pratt Museum. 1896.

Beaudry, Louis N. *War Journal of Louis N. Beaudry, Fifth New York Cavalry.* North Carolina: McFarland and Company. 1996.

Betts, John. "Home Front, Battlefield and Sport during the Civil War." *Research Quarterly.* May 1971.

Biographical Review. Cooperstown, NY: New York State Historical Association. 1893.

Braden, Donna R. *Leisure and Entertainment in America.* Dearborn, Michigan: Henry Ford Museum and Greenfield Village. 1988.

Brown, Louis A. *The Salisbury Prison: A Case Study of Confederate Military Prisons.* Wendell, North Carolina: Avera Press. 1980.

Cauldwell, William. Letter. Mills Papers. Cooperstown, NY: National Baseball Hall of Fame Library. 11 February 1905.

Chilsolm, Julian J. *A Manual of Military Surgery, For the Use of Surgeons in the Confederate Army.* Columbia: Evans and Cogswell. 1864.

Commager, Henry Steele. *The Blue and the Gray.* Indianapolis: The Bobbs-Merrill Company, Inc. 1960.

Cooper, James Fenimore. Samuel Shaw. Walter R. Littell. Harold H. Hollis. *A History of Cooperstown.* Cooperstown, NY: New York State Historical Association. 1976.

Crockett, S. "Sports and Recreational Practices of Union and Confederate Soldiers." *Research Quarterly.* October 1961.

Cumming, John. *Runners and Walkers: A Nineteenth Century Sports Chronicle.* Chicago: Regnery Gateway. 1981.

Daniel, Dan. "The Civil War and Baseball." *World Telegram* and *Sun Feature Magazine.* Cooperstown, NY: exhibit at the National Baseball Hall of Fame Library. 1960.

Davies, Wallace Evan. *Patriotism on Parade.* Cambridge: Harvard University Press. 1955.

Dulles, Foster Rhea. *A History of Recreation: America Learns to Play.* New York: Appleton-Century-Crofts. 1965.

Durant, John and Bettmann, Otto. *Pictorial History of American Sports from Colonial Times to the Present.* A. S. Barnes and Company, Inc. 1952.

Durant, John. *The Story of Baseball in words and pictures.* New York: Hastings House. 1947.

Fielding, Lawrence. "Sport and the Terrible Swift Sword." *Research Quarterly.* March 1977.

Fielding, Lawrence. "Sport: The Meter Stick of the Civil War Soldier." *Canadian Journal of History of Sport.* May 1978.

Fink, Ruth W. "Recreational Pursuits in the Old South." *Research Quarterly.* October 1961.

Freeman's Journal, staff of. "A Century of Baseball." Booklet. Cooperstown, NY: *Freeman's Journal.* 1940.

Giamatti, A. Bartlett. Papers. Cooperstown, NY: National Baseball Hall of Fame Library. 17 October 1985.

Gilbert, Tom. *Baseball and the Color Line.* New York: Franklin Watts. 1995.

Glazier, Willard. *The Capture, The Prison Pen and the Escape.* Albany. 1866.

Gorn, Elliot and Warren Goldstein. *A Brief History of American Sports.* Hill and Wang. 1993.

Grant, Ulysses, S. *Personal Memoirs of U. S. Grant.* New York: Dover Publications. 1995.

Hakim, Joy. *War, Terrible War.* New York: Oxford University Press. 1994.

Hanifen, Michael. *History of Battery B First New Jersey Artillery.* Hightstown: Longstreet House. 1905.

Harding, John. Letter. Cooperstown, NY: National Baseball Hall of Fame Library. 1863.

Harper's Weekly. 19th century newspaper. Cooperstown, NY: New York State Historical Association. 1859-1865.

Hawke, David Freeman. *Everyday Life in Early America.* New York: Harper and Row. 1988.

Hawley, Gideon. *Rev. Gideon Hawley's Journal.* Broome County. Collection of Tom Heitz. 1753.

Henderson, Robert W. *Ball, Bat and Bishop.* New York: Rockport Press. 1947.

Henderson, Robert. "Baseball and Rounders." Bulletin of The New York Public Library. Volume 43, number 4. 1939.

Kaminsky, Virginia Hughes. *A War to Petrify the Heart.* Hensonville, New York: Black Dome Press. 1997.

Kirsch, George. *The Creation of American Team Sports.* Urbana: University of Illinois Press. 1989.

Malloy, Jerry. "Early Black Baseball/Charles Douglas." www.erols.com/brak/antebell.html accessed 2 June 1999.

McClintock, Inez and Marshall. *Toys in America.* Washington, D.C.: Public Affairs Office. 1961.

McDonald, Forest. *Cracker Culture.* Tuscaloosa: The University of Alabama Press. 1988.

Merrifield, Andrew S. Papers. Cooperstown, NY: National Baseball Hall of Fame Library. (no date).

Millen, Patricia. Unpublished paper. 1997.

Mills, A. G. "The Evening World's Baseball Panorama." Mills Papers. Cooperstown, NY: National Baseball Hall of Fame Library. 1923.

Mitchell, Reid. *Civil War Soldiers.* New York: Viking Press. 1988.

Porter's Spirit of the Times. 19th century newspaper. New York: William T. Porter. 1856-1857.

Rawlings, Kevin. "Christmas in the Civil War." *Civil War Times*. December 1998.

Rolfe, George. Diary. Copy by Ted Shuart from the Albany State Library, NY. 1864.

Salvatore, Victor. "Abner's False Rep." *Eastern Review*. August, 1983.

Seymour, Harold. *Baseball: The Early Years*. New York: Oxford University Press. 1960.

Seymour, Harold. *Baseball: The People's Game*. New York: Oxford University Press. 1990.

Smith, Robert. *Baseball*. New York: Simon and Schuster. 1947.

Spalding, Albert G. *America's National Game: Baseball*. San Francisco: Halo Books. 1991.

Spalding's Official Baseball Guide. Cooperstown, NY: National Baseball Hall of Fame Library. 1908.

Spivey, Donald. *Sport in America: New Historical Perspectives*. Westport, Connecticut: Greenwood Press. 1985.

Sullivan, Dean A. *Early Innings*. Lincoln and London: University of Nebraska Press. 1995.

Sumner, Jim. "POWs Collected RBIs in Civil War Prison Camp." *Baseball America*. Civil War file. Cooperstown, NY: National Baseball Hall of Fame Library. 1997.

Sumner, Jim. "Baseball at Salisbury Prison Camp." *Baseball History*. Westport, CT: Meckler. 1989.

Sutherland, Daniel E. *The Expansion of Everyday Life*. New York: Harper and Row. 1989.

"The Game Endures: A Civil War Diary." *Humanities*. Vol. 15, No. 4. 1994.

The New York Clipper. Cooperstown, NY: National Baseball Hall of Fame Library. 1860-1869.

The New York Times. January 29, 1893.

Thomas, Emory. *The Confederate Nation*. New York: Harper Torchbooks. 1979.

Thomas, Mrs. William B. Letter. Cooperstown, NY: National Baseball Hall of Fame Library. 1989.

Twombly, Wells. *200 Years of Sport in America*. New York: McGraw-Hill Company. 1976.

Voigt, David Quentin. *American Baseball*. Norman: University of Oklahoma Press. 1996.

Ward, Geoffrey and Ken Burns. *Baseball: An Illustrated History*. New York: Alfred A. Knopf. 1994.

Weaver, Robert B. *Amusements and Sports in American Life*. Chicago: The University of Chicago Press. 1939.

"When Town Ball Was the Big Game Here." *The Atlanta Journal*. 9 March 1924.

Wiggins, Kenneth. "Sport and Popular Pastimes in the Plantation Community: The Slave Experience." Thesis. University of Maryland. 1979.

Wiley, Bell Irvin. *The Common Soldier in the Civil War.* New York: Grosset and Dunlap. 1960.

Wilke's Spirit of the Times. 19th century newspaper. New York: George Wilkes. 1860-1861.

Wittke, Dean Carl. "A Hundred Years of Baseball." Mills Papers. Cooperstown, NY: National Baseball Hall of Fame Library. 1939.

Wright, Mike. *What They Didn't Teach You About The Civil War.* Novato, CA: Presidio. 1996.

Zoss, Joel and John Bowman. *Diamonds in the Rough: The Untold History of Baseball.* Contemporary Books. 1996.

Index

TOWNSEND, E D 56
TYLER, 23
VAN WYCK, 12 Richard 12
WARD, John 52

WEBSTER, Daniel 74
WEED, Thurlow 74
WILSON, W B 22
YOUNG, Cy 65

AUTHOR: Patricia Millen Ms. Millen has a BS from the Empire Sta[ ]
College at the State University of New York. The author has he[ ]
positions as Supervisor of Museum Teachers at the New York Sta[ ]
Historical Association in Cooperstown, NY; Museum Cataloger at th[ ]
Senate House State Historic Site in Kingston, NY; Executive Directo[ ]
Curator at the Pratt Museum in Prattsville, NY; and Site Administrator[ ]
The Thomas Clarke House State Historic Site in Princeton, NJ. Awar[ ]
include: the 1995 "Best of New York" for historic preservation from th[ ]
Preservation League of New York; the 1993 Winthrop L. Cart[ ]
Memorial Grant from the Early American Industries Association [ ]
Wilmington; and the 1992 Historic Preservation Award from Greer[ ]
County Legislature (NY).

Ms. Millen's previous publications include her book *Bare Tree[ ]
Zadock Pratt Master Tanner and The Story of What Happened to t[ ]
Catskill Mountain Forests* (Black Dome Press, NY. 1995), and numero[ ]
published articles on 19th century American history. A Civil W[ ]
enthusiast, she became interested in the connection between baseball ar[ ]
the war while living in Cooperstown, New York. Patricia now lives wi[ ]
her family in Titusville, New Jersey.

www.ingramcontent.com/pod-product-compliance
Lightning Source LLC
Chambersburg PA
CBHW052107090426
42741CB00009B/1713